The World Cup

The World Cup

The Players, Coaches, History, and Excitement

A FRIEDMAN GROUP BOOK

Published by MALLARD PRESS
An imprint of BDD Promotional Book Company, Inc.
666 Fifth Avenue
New York, New York 10103

Mallard Press and its accompanying design and logo are trademarks of BDD Promotional Book Company, Inc.

IBSN 0-792-45314-X

THE WORLD CUP
The Players, Coaches, History, and Excitement
was prepared and produced by
Michael Friedman Publishing Group, Inc.
15 West 26th Street
New York, New York 10010

Editor: Sharon Kalman
Art Director/Designer: Jeff Batzli
Photo Researcher: Daniella Jo Nilva

Typset by: The Interface Group, Inc.
Color separations by Scantrans Pte. Ltd.
Printed and bound in Hong Kong by Leefung-Asco Printers Ltd.

Dedicated to my Czech father, Ota, who taught me this sport; and to my very American children, Stefan and Halley, who keep the ball rolling.

Contents

CHAPTER ONE
The Matches 6

CHAPTER TWO
The Players 48

CHAPTER THREE
The Countries 98

©David Cannon/Allsport

©Vandystadt/Allsport

©Vandystadt/Allsport

CHAPTER ONE
The Matches

The French have never won the World Cup, but they can lay claim to its invention and cultivation. The first seed was planted in Paris, in 1904, at the inaugural meeting of FIFA (Federation Internationale des Football Associations). Here, it was declared, the organization of soccer-playing nations would someday create a world championship.

THE WORLD CUP CONCEIVED

AFTER TWO DECADES OF INFIGHTING AND CONSIDERABLE procrastination, FIFA met again in 1924 at the Paris Olympics to sketch out details for the first World Cup. In fact, the World Cup tournament might never have evolved if the Olympics had allowed professional soccer players to compete. But since this was not to be, FIFA recognized the need for a showcase soccer tournament that would not penalize the European nations and their paraprofessionals. (The Olympic Committee has recently ruled that, beginning in 1992, all players must be under twenty-three years old.) The two Frenchmen who steered this tournament from conception to the playing fields of Uruguay in 1930 were Henri Delauney, secretary of FIFA, and president Jules Rimet, for whom the trophy awarded to the winning team was later named.

By the 1928 Olympics in Amsterdam, FIFA was ready to award the World Cup to a worthy host for 1930. Five nations put in their bids: Holland, Italy, Spain, Sweden, and Uruguay. Uruguay, wanting to celebrate its 100th anniversary of independence with great flourish, agreed to foot the travel and hotel bills of all visiting teams and to build a new stadium expressly for the World Cup. This was an offer Rimet and FIFA could not refuse; however, the other four bidding countries were unhappy with the outcome and, as a result, the four losing bidders boycotted the first World Cup, as did England, Hungary, Germany, Switzerland, and Czechoslovakia.

From a historical perspective, it would be their loss.

The FIFA World Cup trophy, which replaced the Jules Rimet Cup. There have been prettier trophies, certainly, but none more valued.

© Vandystadt/Allsport

WORLD CUP I: URUGUAY, 1930

THE FIRST WORLD CUP WAS A SLAPDASH THIRTEEN-NATION AFFAIR, with last-minute entrants and a long, arduous boat journey across the Atlantic for the four European squads that agreed to participate: Belgium, France, Yugoslavia, and Romania. The Romanians were an odd lot, selected from company teams and afforded month-long vacations by no less than King Carol himself. (Most World Cup players are picked by a national selection committee, usually including the nation's coach, manager, and "technical directors.")

Without the presence of Italy, Austria, Holland, Spain, Sweden, Czechoslovakia, England, or Holland, Uruguay became the heavy favorite by default. After all, it had won gold medals at the 1924 and 1928 Olympics, and had some truly creative attackers from midfield: forward Pedro Cea, and halfbacks Lorenzo Fernandez, Jose Andrade, and Alvaro Gestido.

Among the thirteen teams that attended this inaugural event was the United States, which fielded a side of foreign-born players strong enough to dominate weak members Paraguay and Belgium.

Matches were not always top-flight, but usually competitive, and Montevideo responded with unreined enthusiasm. Individual players like rough-and-tumble center-half Luisito Monti and center-forward Guillermo Stabile of Argentina, not well known outside of their own countries, became two of the world's first international sports stars.

Argentina, Uruguay's chief rival, seemed to court controversy and chaos: With France trailing Argentina 1–0, and with Marcel Langiller on a breakneck dribble toward the goal, Brazilian ref Almeida Rego stopped the game with his whistle. Rego incorrectly believed time had run out when there were still six minutes remaining. The match resumed, but Langiller no longer had his chance and Argentina held on. In the Argentinians' next match against Mexico, a Bolivian official called five penalty kicks. Their final Group 1 match against Chile was interrupted by a lengthy brawl caused by one of Monti's patented loose tackles.

Finally, after knocking off the United States 6–1, Argentina earned passage into the first final against Uruguay. A crowd of 90,000 poured into Centenary Stadium, many of them Argentinians who had caught a boat across the Plate River on the eve of the match. Uruguay won a coin toss, which allowed the team to use its

THE FIRST WORLD CUP WAS A SLAPDASH THIRTEEN-NATION AFFAIR, WITH LAST-MINUTE ENTRANTS AND A LONG, ARDUOUS BOAT JOURNEY ACROSS THE ATLANTIC.

© Bettmann/Hulton

The first World Cup went to Uruguay, the spurned hosts. Here, Lorenzo Fernandez, Pedro Cea, and Hector Scarone celebrate a 4–2 comeback win over Argentina.

own native soccer ball in the first half. Down 2–1 at intermission, the Uruguayans looked to their top scorer, Cea. He responded with a neat bit of footwork and the tying goal at fifty-five minutes, and Uruguay caught fire. Goals by Santos Iriarte and Hector Castro clinched the 4–2 victory, and the first World Cup. The overflow crowd behaved in exemplary fashion: not necessarily a portent of the raucous future.

1930 · Uruguay

GROUP 1

France (3) 4 **Mexico** (0) 1
(Laurent, Langiller, Maschinot 2) *(Carreno)*

Argentina (0) 1 **France** (0) 0
(Monti)

Chile (1) 3 **Mexico** (0) 0
(Vidal, Subiabre 2)

Chile (0) 1 **France** (0) 0
(Subiabre)

Argentina (3) 6 **Mexico** (0) 3
(Stabile 3, Varallo 2, Zumelzu) *(Lopez, Rosas F., Rosas M.)*

Argentina (2) 3 **Chile** (1) 1
(Stabile 2, Evaristo M.) *(Subiabre)*

	GP	W	D	L	GF	GA	Pts
Argentina	3	3	0	0	10	4	6
Chile	3	2	0	1	5	3	4
France	3	1	0	2	4	3	2
Mexico	3	0	0	3	4	13	0

GROUP 2

Yugoslavia (2) 2 **Brazil** (0) 1
(Tirnanic, Beck) *(Neto)*

Yugoslavia (1) 4 **Bolivia** (0) 0
(Beck 2, Marianovic, Vujadinovic)

Brazil (1) 4 **Bolivia** (0) 0
(Visintainer 2, Neto 2)

	GP	W	D	L	GF	GA	Pts
Yugoslavia	2	2	0	0	6	1	4
Brazil	2	1	0	1	5	2	2
Bolivia	2	0	0	2	0	8	0

GROUP 3

Romania (1) 3 **Peru** (0) 1
(Staucin 2, Barbu) *(Souza)*

Uruguay (0) 1 **Peru** (0) 0
(Castro)

Uruguay (4) 4 **Romania** (0) 0
(Dorado, Scarone, Anselmo, Cea)

	GP	W	D	L	GF	GA	Pts
Uruguay	2	2	0	0	5	0	4
Romania	2	1	0	1	3	5	2
Peru	2	0	0	2	1	4	0

GROUP 4

USA (2) 3 **Belgium** (0) 0
(McGhee 2, Patenaude)

USA (2) 3 **Paraguay** (0) 0
(Patenaude 2, Florie)

Paraguay (1) 1 **Belgium** (0) 0
(Pena)

	GP	W	D	L	GF	GA	Pts
USA	2	2	0	0	6	0	4
Paraguay	2	1	0	1	1	3	2
Belgium	2	0	0	2	0	4	0

SEMIFINALS

Argentina (1) 6 **USA** (0) 1
(Monti, Scopelli, Stabile 2, Peucelle 2) *(Brown)*

Uruguay (3) 6 **Yugoslavia** (1) 1
(Cea 3, Anselmo 2, Iriarte) *(Seculic)*

FINAL *(Montevideo, 7/30/30)*

Uruguay (1) 4 **Argentina** (2) 2
(Dorado, Cea, Iriarte, Castro) *(Peucelle, Stabile)*

Uruguay: Ballesteros; Nasazzi, Mascheroni; Andrade, Fernandez, Gestido; Dorado, Scarone, Castro, Cea, Iriarte

Argentina: Botosso; Della Toree, Paternoster; Evaristo, J., Monti, Suarez; Peucelle, Varallo, Stabile, Ferreira, Evaristo, M.

Referee: *Langenus (Belgium)*

Never graceful, always willing, the United States soccer team trained against the University of Pennsylvania in preparation for the 1934 tournament. The Americans were not quite ready for host Italy, and were humbled, 7–1.

WORLD CUP II: ITALY, 1934

BENITO MUSSOLINI WANTED AN INTERNATIONAL SHOWCASE, AND this would be it: The second World Cup, headquartered in Rome. His presence pervaded the matches and he did everything but order his favored Italian squad to don brown shirts. The traditional blues, or "Mussolini's azzurris," would have to do.

Needless to say, there was some ill feeling about the fascist pomp, and the defending champion Uruguayans declined to participate. A strong sixteen-nation field (the standard number of teams for the next forty-eight years) entered the one-loss elimination tournament, and the final eight sides were all from Europe.

In the first round, the Italians dismantled a weak American team 7–1. France was the greatest surprise, playing Austria even at Turin before losing 3–2, in part because of an obvious offside goal by inside left Schall. French fans contended for years that referee Van Moorsel of Holland had been distracted by news of the Dutch team being eliminated by Switzerland.

Matters grew uglier in the second round, the quarterfinals. Italy came back to tie Spain 1–1. Zamora and six of his teammates were injured and missed the replay the next day. The Italians knocked out three more players, two of Spain's goals were nullified, and Italy finally won 1–0. The Swiss referee Mercet was later suspended for his shameless inaction in that replay.

Next, Italy nipped Austria 1–0 in the heavy rain of Milan, conditions which neutralized the Austrians' neat, short passing game. The Italians' opponents in the final, surprisingly, were the underrated Czechs, who had relied on the goaltending prowess of captain Franticek Planicka to defeat Germany.

The final was a match between the Italians' power and discipline, honed by famed coach Vittorio Pozzo, and the Czechs' more delicate skills. The Czechs pushed ahead 1–0 with twenty minutes left in regulation play on a goal that developed on the left wing. But Mussolini's blue shirts were rescued when Raimondo Orsi—an Argentinian playing for Italy—curled a goal past Planicka with eight minutes left. In overtime, Italian forward Schiavio dribbled past one defender and beat Planicka for the winner.

Mussolini's show was complete. Later, he moved onto another stage, where the Italians would meet with less success.

© Bettmann/Hulton

Before the final against Czechoslovakia, the Italian players gave a fascist salute to partisan spectator Benito Mussolini. For eighty-two minutes, before the Italians pulled off the win, Mussolini squirmed in his box.

1934 · Italy

FIRST ROUND

Italy (3)7	**USA** (0)1		
(Schiavio 3, Orsi 2,	*(Donelli)*		
Meazza, Ferrari)			
Czech. (0)2	**Romania** (1)1		
(Puc, Nejedly)	*(Dobai)*		
Germany (1)5	**Belgium** (2)2		
(Conen 3,	*(Voorhoof 2)*		
Kobierski 2)			
Austria (1)(1)3	**France** *(1)(1)2		
(Sindelar, Schall,	*Nicholas,*		
Bican)	*Verriest*)*		
Spain (3)3	**Brazil** (1)1		
(Iraragorri,*	*(Silva)*		
Langara 2)			
Switzerland(2)3	**Netherlands**(1)2		
(Kielholz 2,	*(Smit, Vente)*		
Abegglen)			
Sweden (1)3	**Argentina** (1)2		
(Jonasson 2,	*(Belis, Galateo)*		
Kroon)			
Hungary (2)4	**Egypt** (1)2		
(Teleky, Toldi 2,	*(Fawzi 2)*		
Vincze)			

*Penalty kick goal

SECOND ROUND

Germany (1)2	**Sweden** (0)1		
(Hohmann 2)	*(Dunker)*		
Austria (1)2	**Hungary** (0)1		
(Horwath,	*(Sarosi)*		
Zischek)			
Italy (0)(1)1	**Spain** (1)(1)1		
(Ferrari)	*(Regueiro)*		
Italy (1)1	**Spain** (0)0		
(Meazza)			
Czech. (1)3	**Switzerland**(1)2		
(Svoboda, Sobotka,	*(Kielholz, Abeg-*		
Nejedly)	*glen)*		

SEMIFINALS

Czech. (1)3	**Germany** (0)1		
(Nejedly 2, Krcil)	*(Noack)*		
Italy (1)1	**Austria** (0)0		
(Guaita)			

THIRD PLACE GAME *(Naples)*

Germany (3)3	**Austria** (1)2		
(Lehner 2, Conen)	*(Horwath, Seszta)*		

FINAL *(Rome, 6/10/34)*

Italy (0)(1)2	**Czech.** (0)(1)1		
(Orsi, Schiavio)	*(Puc)*		

Italy: Combi; Monzeglio, Allemandi; Ferraris, Monti, Bertolini; Guaita, Meazza, Schiavio, Ferrari, Orsi
Czechoslovakia: Planicka; Zenisek, Ctyroky; Kostalek, Cambal, Krcil; Junek, Svoboda, Sobotka, Nejedly, Puc

Referee: Eklind (Sweden)

A second title for soccer genius and provocateur, Italian manager Vittorio Pozzo.

© Bettmann/Hulton

WORLD CUP III: *FRANCE, 1938*

THE MATCH IN MARSEILLES STADIUM WAS DELAYED A FEW MINUTES BY AN INTERMINABLE STRAIGHT-ARM SALUTE BY POZZO, TAUNTING THE ANTI-FASCIST CROWD DURING PRE-GAME CEREMONIES.

WORLD WAR II WAS RIGHT AROUND THE CORNER NOW, AND AUSTRIA had already been engulfed, its vaunted soccer teams plundered by the Germans. A revamped Italian team, still under Pozzo's stern command, was favored to win with its young star, center forward Silvio Piola, as the creative force.

In the very first round of the elimination tournament, however, the Italians were nearly beaten by upstart Norway. The match in Marseilles Stadium was delayed a few minutes by an interminable straight-arm salute by Pozzo, taunting the anti-fascist crowd during pre-game ceremonies. With the match tied 1–1 late in the second half, Aldo Olivieri made a legendary one-handed save on a dead-on shot that would have been the decisive score. Instead, Piola scored five minutes into overtime on a rebound.

Czechoslovakia, a finalist in 1934, was not as fortunate in the second round. It played a wild match against Brazil, a team with enormous but unbridled talent. Czech attacker Nejedly was kicked and injured early by Brazilian Zeze, who was tossed from the game. Two other players—one from each side—were ejected for fighting. Star goalie Planicka broke his arm. Eventually, the match ended in a 1–1 draw, demanding a replay. The Czechs and Brazilians made a total of fifteen lineup changes because of injuries, suspensions, and bad blood, then went at it again. This time Brazil won 2–1, but both nations were losers. The Czechs were out of the tournament, and Brazil's World Cup reputation was badly tarnished.

Italy knocked off Brazil in the semifinals, 2–1, then faced Hungary in Stade Colombes in Paris. The Italians jumped off to a 3–1 lead at the half, then sealed their second successive World Cup on Piola's goal in the eightieth minute. The Italians had won convincingly, 4–2, and had proven the superiority of Pozzo's rugged, rigid system over the more technically aesthetic styles of the Hungarians, Czechs, and South Americans. The World Cup would now be put on hold for world war, as it had to be.

1938 · France

FIRST ROUND

Swtzrlnd (1)(1)1	**Germany** (0)(1)1			
(Abegglen)	(Gauchel)			
Switzerland (0)4	**Germany** (2)2			
(Wallaschek,	(Hahnemann,			
Bickel,	Loertscher, o.g.)			
Abegglen 2)				
Cuba (0)(2)3	**Romania** (1)(2)3			
(Tunas, Maquina,	(Covaci, Baratki,			
Sosa)	Dobai)			
Cuba (2)2	**Romania** (1)1			
(Socorro,	(Dobai)			
Maquina)				
Hungary (4)6	**Dutch E.**			
(Kohut, Toldi,	**Indies** (0)0			
Sarosi 2,				
Zsengeller 2)				
France (2)3	**Belgium** (1)1			
(Vienante,	(Isemborghs)			
Nicolas 2)				
Czech (0)(0)3	**Nethrlnds**(0)(0)0			
(Kostalek, Boucek,				
Nejedly)				
Brazil (3)(4)6	**Poland** (1)(4)5			
(Leonidas 4,	(Willimowski 4,			
Peracio,	Piontek)			
Romeu)				
Italy (1)(1)2	**Norway** (0)(1)1			
(Ferrari, Piola)	(Brustad)			

SECOND ROUND

Sweden (4)8	**Cuba** (0)0			
(Andersson,				
Jonasson,				
Wetterstroem 4,				
Nyberg, Keller)				
Hungary (1)2	**Switzerland** (0)0			
(Zsengeller 2)				
Italy (1)3	**France** (1)1			
(Colaussi, Piola 2)	(Heisserer)			
Brazil (1)(1)1	**Czech** (0)(1)1			
(Leonidas)	(Nejedly*)			
Brazil (0)2	**Czech** (1)1			
(Leonidas,	(Kopecky)			
Roberto)				

SEMIFINALS

Italy (2)2	**Brazil** (0)1			
(Colaussi,	(Romeu)			
Meazza*)				
Hungary (3)5	**Sweden** (1)1			
(Zsengeller 3,	(Nyberg)			
Titkos, Sarosi)				

THIRD PLACE GAME (Bordeaux)

Brazil (1)4	**Sweden** (2)2			
(Romeu, Leonidas	(Jonasson,			
2, Peracio)	Nyberg)			

FINAL (Paris, 6/19/38)

Italy (3)4	**Hungary** (1)2			
(Colaussi 2,	(Titkos, Sarosi)			
Piola 2)				

Italy: Olivieri; Foni, Rava; Serantoni, Andreolo, Locatelli; Biavati, Meazza, Piola, Ferrari, Colaussi

Hungary: Szabo; Polger, Biro; Szalay, Szucs, Lazar; Sas, Vincze, Sarosi, Zsengeller, Titkos

Referee: Capdeville (France)

*Penalty kick goal

WORLD CUP IV: *BRAZIL, 1950*

THE FOURTH WORLD CUP BEGAN AS SOMETHING OF A DISASTER, BUT ended with a purity of spirit and athleticism in a memorable final. Organizers used every inch of their enormous country to demoralize visiting nations, it seemed, scheduling them to play in a remote northern stadium one day, then in another southern site 2,000 miles (3,200 km) away. The showcase coliseum, Maracana Stadium, seated 200,000, but was not quite completed for opening day.

Most of the top teams competed, including first-time participant England. The English had been considered the equal of Italy before the war, and now they were labeled the European equivalent of

IN THE LITTLE STADIUM OF BELO HORIZONTE, THE UNITED STATES PULLED OFF A 1-0 VICTORY THAT ABSOLUTELY NOBODY HAD ANTICIPATED.

Brazil. This made their second match (the tournament returned to a group format, instead of single elimination) all the more stunning. In the little stadium of Belo Horizonte, the United States pulled off a 1–0 victory that absolutely nobody had anticipated or could explain. England hit crossbar and post, attacking all afternoon against a mix of native Americans and foreign imports. But the English couldn't score. In the thirty-seventh minute, Joe Gaetjens, a Haitian-American, headed Walter Bahr's cross into the net.

"At the time, I didn't think anything about it, because it was so early in the game," American fullback Harry Keough, from St. Louis, Missouri, would say years later. "I figured we just woke up the sleeping giant."

But the American defense held firm under pressure, and back in England no period of mourning was deemed sufficient for such tragedy.

Eventually, Brazil and Uruguay met in the match that decided the World Cup; one that, because of the strange format—a final pool of four teams in a round-robin playoff—the Brazilians needed only to tie in front of their rabid home fans. The local governor gave a long-winded speech declaring the Brazilians inevitable victors before the match, and Friaca seemed to decide matters with his goal from the right side in the forty-seventh minute. But the Uruguayans put their short-passing game in order, freeing the graceful inside-left Juan Schiaffino on a cross from right wing Chico Ghiggia. Schiaffino tied the score 1–1 in the sixty-fifth minute. With eleven minutes left, Ghiggia freed himself on a simple give-and-go, dribbled the ball inside, and beat Brazilian goaltender Barbosa to the near post for the winner.

Back in Montevideo, six Uruguayan fans died from excitement at this unexpected victory over the Brazilians. Uruguay had won the World Cup for the second time, tying Italy for top honors.

The United States team poses at Randalls Island, New York, one day before departing for Brazil and an upset over England. Front row (from left): Jeff Combs, Nick D. Orio, Adal Molanin, Gino Gardassanish, Gino Pariani, Robert Anni, Walter Bahr. Second row (from left): Robert Graddock, Frank Borghi, Joe Maca, Ed Souza, John Souza. Rear (from left): Chubby Lyon, Frank Valecenti, Joe Gaetjens, Charles Colombo, Harry Keough, coach Bill Jeffy.

1950 · Brazil

GROUP 1

Brazil (1)4 **Mexico** (0)0
(Ademir 2, Jair,
Baltazar)
Yugoslavia (3)3 **Switzerland** (0)0
(Tomasevic 2,
Ognanov)
Yugoslavia (2)4 **Mexico** (0)1
(Bobek, (Casarin)
Cajkowski II 2,
Tomasevic)
Brazil (1)2 **Switzerland** (1)2
(Alfredo, Baltazar) (Fatton, Tamini)
Brazil (1)2 **Yugoslavia** (0)0
(Ademir, Zizinho)
Switzerlnd (2)2 **Mexico** (0)1
(Bader, Fatton) (Velasquez)

	GP	W	D	L	GF	GA	Pts
Brazil	3	2	1	0	8	2	5
Yugoslavia	3	2	0	1	7	3	4
Switzerland	3	1	1	1	4	6	3
Mexico	3	0	0	3	2	10	0

GROUP 2

Spain (0)3 **USA** (1)1
(Basora 2, Zarra) (Souza, J.)
England (1)2 **Chile** (0)0
(Mortensen,
Mannion)
USA (1)1 **England** (0)0
(Gaetjens)
Spain (2)2 **Chile** (0)0
(Basora, Zarra)

Spain (0)1 **England** (0)0
(Zarra)
Chile (2)5 **USA** (0)2
(Robledo, (Pariani,
Cremaschi 3, Souza, J.)
Prieto)

	GP	W	D	L	GF	GA	Pts
Spain	3	3	0	0	6	1	6
England	3	1	0	2	2	2	2
Chile	3	1	0	2	5	6	2
USA	3	1	0	2	4	8	2

GROUP 3

Sweden (2)3 **Italy** (1)2
(Jeppson 2, (Carapellese,
Andersson) Muccinelli)
Sweden (2)2 **Paraguay** (1)2
(Sundqvist, (Lopez, A.,
Palmer) Lopez, F.)
Italy (1)2 **Paraguay** (0)0
(Carapellese,
Pandolfini)

	GP	W	D	L	GF	GA	Pts
Sweden	2	1	1	0	5	4	3
Italy	2	1	0	1	4	3	2
Paraguay	2	0	1	1	2	4	1

GROUP 4

Uruguay (4)8 **Bolivia** (0)0
(Schiaffino 4,
Miguez 2, Vidal,
Ghiggia)

	GP	W	D	L	GF	GA	Pts
Uruguay	1	1	0	0	8	0	2
Bolivia	1	0	0	1	0	8	0

FINAL POOL

Uruguay (1)2 **Spain** (2)2
(Ghiggia, Varela) (Basora 2)
Brazil (3)7 **Sweden** (0)1
(Ademir 4, (Andersson*)
Chico 2, Maneca)
Uruguay (1)3 **Sweden** (2)2
(Ghiggia, (Palmer,
Miguez 2) Sundqvist)
Brazil (3)6 **Spain** (0)1
(Jair 2, Chico 2, (Igoa)
Zizinho,
Parra, o.g.)
Sweden (2)3 **Spain** (0)1
(Johnsson, (Zarra)
Mellberg, Palmer)
Uruguay (0)2 **Brazil** (0)1
(Schiaffino, (Friaca)
Ghiggia)
(Deciding match played at Rio de
Janeiro, 7/16/50)

	GP	W	D	L	GF	GA	Pts
Uruguay	3	2	1	0	7	5	5
Brazil	3	2	0	1	14	4	4
Sweden	3	1	0	2	6	11	2
Spain	3	0	1	2	4	11	1

Uruguay: Maspoli; Gonzales, Tejera;
Gambretta, Varela, Andrade; Ghiggia,
Perez, Miguez, Schiaffino, Moran
Brazil: Barbosa; Augusto, Juvenal;
Bauer, Banilo, Bigode; Friaca, Zizinho,
Ademir, Jair, Chico

*Penalty kick goal

Referee: Reader (England)

WORLD CUP V: SWITZERLAND, 1954

THE SPORT OF SOCCER HAD BY NOW REACHED ANOTHER LEVEL OF popularity, followed with utter fanaticism by newspaper readers, radio listeners, and even a few television watchers in a relatively peaceful world. With this explosion came superior athletes with superior mobility. No nation embodied this new surge of talent more than Hungary, the class team of the fifth World Cup.

The Hungarians had embarrassed England 6–3 and 7–1 in full internationals (exhibition matches played between nations) leading to the World Cup. They were led by attackers Ferenc Puskas, captain and powerful left-footed scorer; Josef Bozsik, a battler and instinctive player; and Sandor Kocsis, a nimble man with great quickness and ball-hawking flair. In yet another odd configuration, the tournament was divided into four groups of four teams, with two seeded teams in each group who would not play each other.

The Hungarians scored seventeen goals in their first two matches, including a decisive 8–3 victory over the West Germans—

THE HUNGARIANS SCORED SEVENTEEN GOALS IN THEIR FIRST TWO MATCHES…MAKING THEIR RETURN TO WORLD CUP PLAY AFTER SIXTEEN YEARS AND THE DEVASTATION OF WORLD WAR.

Uruguay goalkeeper Maspolo agonizes while Austria celebrates a goal. The roughhouse South Americans finished fourth, while the best team, Hungary, took second.

making their return to World Cup play after sixteen years and the devastation of world war. In that victory, however, Puskas was seriously hurt on a sloppy tackle by center-half Werner Liebrich.

In the quarterfinals, a match dubbed "The Battle of Berne," Hungary and Brazil staged an all-out war without the ailing Puskas. The Hungarians scored two goals quickly, and eventually won 4–2. But this commonplace score belied the activities on and off the field. There were three ejections, forty-two free kicks, four cautions, and two penalty kicks. Referee Arthur Ellis of England endured constant abuse from the fans, from the laughing, taunting players, and later from the Brazilian media. When the match was over, a melee between the two teams in the dressing rooms resulted in a three-inch (8-cm) gash to the face of Brazil's Pinheiro. Puskas was blamed for smashing a bottle to Pinheiro's head, but this was never proven.

Understandably drained by all this, the Hungarians faced Germany again in the final, believing the match to be no more than a formality. Puskas played, scoring a goal despite his nagging ankle injury. Hungary galloped to their customary 2–0 lead, but this time Germany would not fold. Max Morlock and Helmut Rahn scored before the half to equalize. Rahn, an oversized right wing, beat Hungarian goalie Gyula Grosics off a cross from Hans Schaefer. A potential tying goal by Puskas was disallowed by an offside, and German goalie Toni Turek held firm to the 3–2 victory despite a distracting downpour and the rain of Hungary's desperate shots. The innovative Hungarians, like the Dutch some twenty years later, were doomed to be the uncrowned kings of their sport.

1954 · Switzerland

GROUP 1

Yugoslavia (1)1 **France** (0)0
(Milutinovic)

Brazil (4)5 **Mexico** (0)0
(Baltazar, Didi,
Pinga 2, Julinho)

France (1)3 **Mexico** (0)2
(Vincent,   (Naranjo,
Cardenas, o.g.,   Balcazar)
Kopa*)

Brazil (0)(1)1 **Yugoslv** (0)(1)1
(Didi)   (Zebec)

	GP	W	D	L	GF	GA	Pts
Brazil	2	1	1	0	6	1	3
Yugoslavia	2	1	1	0	2	1	3
France	2	1	0	1	3	3	2
Mexico	2	0	0	2	2	8	0

GROUP 2

Hungary (4)9 **Rep. Korea** (0)0
(Czibor, Kocsis 3,
Puskas 2, Lantos,
Palotas 2)

German FR (1)4 **Turkey** (1)1
(Klodt, Morlock,   (Suat)
Schaefer,
Walter, O.)

Hungary (3)8 **German FR** (1)3
(Hidegkuti 2,   (Pfaff, Hermann,
Kocsis   Rahn)
4, Puskas, Toth)

Turkey (4)7 **Rep. Korea** (0)0
Burhan 3, Erol,
Lefter, Suat 2)

	GP	W	D	L	GF	GA	Pts
Hungary	2	2	0	0	17	3	4
German FR	2	1	0	1	7	9	2
Turkey	2	1	0	1	8	4	2
Rep. Korea	2	0	0	2	0	16	0

PLAYOFF

German FR (3)7 **Turkey** (1)2
(Morlock 3,   (Mustafa, Lefter)
Walter, O.,
Walter, F.,
Schaefer 2)

GROUP 3

Austria (1)1 **Scotland** (0)0
(Probst)

Uruguay (0)2 **Czech** (0)0
(Miguez,
Schiaffino)

Austria (4)5 **Czech** (0)0
(Stojaspal 2,
Probst 3)

Uruguay (2)7 **Scotland** (0)0
(Borges 3,
Miguez 2,
Abbadie 2)

	GP	W	D	L	GF	GA	Pts
Uruguay	2	2	0	0	9	0	4
Austria	2	2	0	0	6	0	4
Czechoslovakia	2	0	0	2	0	7	0
Scotland	2	0	0	2	0	8	0

GROUP 4

England (2)(3)4 **Belgium** (1)(3)4
(Broadis 2,   (Anoul 2,
Lofthouse 2)   Coppens,
                   Dickinson, o.g.)

Switzerland (1)2 **Italy** (1)1
(Ballaman, Hugi)   (Boniperti)

England (1)2 **Switzerland** (0)0
(Mullen, Wilshaw)

Italy (1)4 **Belgium** (0)1
(Pandolfini*, Galli,   (Anoul)
Frignani, Lorenzi)

	GP	W	D	L	GF	GA	Pts
England	2	1	1	0	6	4	3
Switzerland	2	1	0	1	2	3	2
Italy	2	1	0	1	2	3	2
Belgium	2	0	1	1	5	8	1

PLAYOFF

Switzerland (1)4 **Italy** (0)1
(Hugi 2, Ballaman,   (Nesti)
Fatton)

QUARTERFINALS

German FR (1)2 **Yugoslavia** (0)0
(Horvat, o.g.,
Rahn)

Hungary (2)4 **Brazil** (1)2
(Hidegkuti,   (Santos, D.*,
Kocsis 2,   Julinho)
Lantos*)

Austria (5)7 **Switzerland** (4)5
(Koerner, A. 2,   (Ballaman 2,
Ocwirk,   Hugi 2,
Wagner 3,   Hanappi, o.g.)
Probst)

Uruguay (2)4 **England** (1)2
(Borges, Varela,   (Lofthouse,
Schiaffino,   Finney)
Ambrois)

SEMIFINALS

German FR (1)6 **Austria** (0)1
(Schaefer,   (Probst)
Morlock,
Walter, F. 2**,
Walter, O. 2)

Hungary (1)(2)4 **Uruguay** (0)(2)2
(Czibor, Hidegkuti,   (Hohberg 2)
Kocsis 2)

THIRD PLACE GAME

Austria (1)3 **Uruguay** (1)1
(Stojaspal*,   (Hohberg)
Cruz, o.g.,
Ocwirk)

FINAL (Berne, 7/4/54)

German FR (2)3 **Hungary** (2)2
(Morlock, Rahn 2)   (Puskas, Czibor)

German Federal Republic: Turek;
Posipal, Kohlmeyer; Eckel, Liebrich,
Mai; Rahn, Morlock, Walter, O., Walter,
F., Schaefer
Hungary: Grosics; Buzansky, Lantos;
Bozsik, Lorant, Zakarias; Czibor,
Kocsis, Hidegkuti, Puskas, Toth

Referee: Ling (England)

*Penalty kick goal

Injustice done: West Germany's Hans Schaefer (20) watches as Helmut Rahn's winning shot beats Hungarian goalie Gyula Grosics. Ailing Hungary lost, 3–2, after beating the Germans 8–3 just two weeks earlier.

WORLD CUP VI: SWEDEN, 1958

PELÉ TRAPPED THE BALL WITH HIS BACK TO THE GOAL, SPUN IT OVER HIS HEAD, THEN KNOCKED IT IN...WITH A THUNDEROUS RIGHT FOOT.

THE 1958 WORLD CUP WAS A SHOWCASE FOR SEVERAL INDIVIDUAL stars, rather than for brilliant soccer. Among the chosen were seventeen-year-old Edson Arantes do Nascimento of Brazil (better known as Pelé), and Just Fontaine of France. Of the two, obviously, Pelé was the more enduring talent, but for nearly two otherwise uneventful weeks, their performances were equally stellar.

Fontaine, paired with the brilliant playmaker Raymond Kopa, expected to be only a reserve on the French team. But when Rene Bliard was injured in practice, Fontaine, a sturdy fireplug and strong finisher, won his starting spot. Fontaine scored three goals against Paraguay in a first-round match, and tallied at least one in every game he played. He finished with a record thirteen goals.

The Brazilians, meanwhile, relied not only on Pelé. They were a sound team, experimenting with a creative 4–2–4 formation under mentor Vicente Feola. Since many of Hungary's stars had defected after the 1956 revolution, Brazil was rightfully considered the pre-tournament favorite. Their flamboyant players, with wondrously outrageous names like Vava, and Didi, were forging a new, technically purer South American style that shaped the decade.

Brazil's quarterfinal match against Wales in Gothenburg was possibly its toughest. The iron Welsh defense held firm until the sixty-sixth minute, when Pelé's shot was unintentionally deflected by captain Stuart Williams into his own net for a 1–0 Brazil victory. The semifinal against France was easier, as Pelé, the teenage phenom, ran amok for three goals in a 5–2 win.

Now came the final, against a surprising host team from Sweden that had reunited its estranged professional stars before the tournament. The Swedes had broken with usual decorum by bringing cheerleaders in during their semifinal victory over West Germany. In the final at Stockholm, however, there were no such diversions, not much enthusiasm, and only a steady rain.

The Swedes scored early, in the fourth minute, on a goal manufactured by the great Gunnar Gren. Vava scored twice, however, and Pelé produced the backbreaking score ten minutes into the second half. Pelé trapped the ball with his back to the goal, spun it over his head, then knocked it in from ten yards (9 m) out with a thunderous right foot. Brazil won 5–2, and finally earned recognition as more than just the bad boys of Berne and Bordeaux.

© Pressens Bild/Allsport

Edson Arantes do Nascimento, already known to the world as the great Pelé, streaks down field for one of two goals in the final at Stockholm. Brazil won, 5–2, and a legend was born.

1958 · Sweden

GROUP 1

German FR (2)**3** **Argentina** (1)**1**
(Rahn 2, Schmidt) (Corbatta)
N. Ireland (1)**1** **Czech** (0)**0**
(Cush)
German FR (1)**2** **Czech** (0)**2**
(Schaefer, Rahn) (Dvorak*, Zikan)
Argentina (1)**3** **N. Ireland** (1)**1**
(Corbatta 2*, (McParland)
Menendez)
German FR (1)**2** **N. Ireland** (1)**2**
(Rahn, Seeler) (McParland 2)
Czech (3)**6** **Argentina** (1)**1**
(Dvorak, Zikan 2, (Corbatta)
Feureisl, Hovorka 2)

	GP	W	D	L	GF	GA	Pts
German FR	3	1	2	0	7	5	4
Czechoslovakia	3	1	1	1	8	4	3
N. Ireland	3	1	1	1	4	5	3
Argentina	3	1	0	2	5	10	2

PLAYOFF

N. Ireland (1)(1)**2** **Czech** (1)(1)**1**
(McParland 2) (Zikan)

GROUP 2

France (2)**7** **Paraguay** (2)**3**
(Fontaine 3, (Amarilla 2*,
Piantoni, Romero)
Kopa, Wisnieski,
Vincent)
Yugoslavia (1)**1** **Scotland** (0)**1**
(Petakovic) (Murray)
Yugoslavia (1)**3** **France** (1)**2**
(Petakovic, (Fontaine 2)
Veselinovic 2)
Paraguay (2)**3** **Scotland** (1)**2**
(Aguero, Re, (Mudie, Collins)
Parodi)
France (2)**2** **Scotland** (0)**1**
(Kopa, Fontaine) (Baird)
Yugoslavia (2)**3** **Paraguay** (1)**3**
(Ognjanovic, (Parodi, Aguero,
Rajkov, Romero)
Veselinovic)

*Penalty kick goal

	GP	W	D	L	GF	GA	Pts
France	3	2	0	1	11	7	4
Yugoslavia	3	1	2	0	7	6	4
Paraguay	3	1	1	1	9	12	3
Scotland	3	0	1	2	4	6	1

GROUP 3

Sweden (1)**3** **Mexico** (0)**0**
(Simonsson 2,
Liedholm*)
Hungary (1)**1** **Wales** (1)**1**
(Bozsik) (Charles, J.)
Wales (1)**1** **Mexico** (1)**1**
(Allchurch) (Belmonte)
Sweden (1)**2** **Hungary** (0)**1**
(Hamrin 2) (Tichy)
Hungary (1)**4** **Mexico** (0)**0**
(Tichy 2, Sandor,
Bencsis)
Sweden (0)**0** **Wales** (0)**0**

	GP	W	D	L	GF	GA	Pts
Sweden	3	2	1	0	5	1	5
Wales	3	0	3	0	2	2	3
Hungary	3	1	1	1	6	3	3
Mexico	3	0	1	2	1	8	1

PLAYOFF

Wales (0)**2** **Hungary** (0)**1**
(Allchurch, (Tichy)
Medwin)

GROUP 4

England (0)**2** **USSR** (1)**2**
(Kevan, Finney*) (Simonian,
Ivanov, A.)
Brazil (1)**3** **Austria** (0)**0**
(Mazzola 2,
Santos, N.)
England (0)**0** **Brazil** (0)**0**
USSR (1)**2** **Austria** (0)**0**
(Ilyin, Ivanov, V.)
Brazil (1)**2** **USSR** (0)**0**
(Vava 2)
England (0)**2** **Austria** (1)**2**
(Haynes, Kevan) (Koller, Koerner)

	GP	W	D	L	GF	GA	Pts
Brazil	3	2	1	0	5	0	5
USSR	3	1	1	1	4	4	3
England	3	0	3	0	4	4	3
Austria	3	0	1	2	2	7	1

PLAYOFF

USSR (0)**1** **England** (0)**0**
(Ilyin)

QUARTERFINALS

France (1)**4** **N. Ireland** (0)**0**
(Wisnieski,
Fontaine
2, Piantoni)
German FR (1)**1** **Yugoslavia** (0)**0**
(Rahn)
Sweden (0)**2** **USSR** (0)**0**
(Hamrin, Simonsson)
Brazil (0)**1** **Wales** (0)**0**
(Pele)

SEMIFINALS

Brazil (2)**5** **France** (1)**2**
(Vava, Didi, (Fontaine, Piantoni)
Pele 3)
Sweden (1)**3** **German FR** (1)**1**
(Skoglund, Gren, (Schaefer)
Hamrin)

THIRD PLACE TEAM *(Gothenburg)

France (0)**6** **German FR** (0)**3**
(Fontaine 4, Kopa*, (Cieslarczyk,
Douis) Rahn, Schaefer)

FINAL (Stockholm, 6/29/58)

Brazil (2)**5** **Sweden** (1)**2**
(Vava 2, Pele 2, (Liedholm,
Zagalo) Simonsson)

Brazil: Glymar; Santos, D., Santos, N.;
Zito, Bellini, Orlando; Garrincha, Didi,
Vava, Pele, Zagalo
Sweden: Svensson; Bergmark, Axbom;
Boerjesson, Gustavsson, Parling; Hamrin,
Gren, Simonsson, Liedholm, Skoglund

Referee: Guigue (France)

WORLD CUP VII: CHILE, 1962

Brazil, now the unchallenged kings of soccer, toppled Czechoslovakia, 3–1, and retired the Jules Rimet Trophy with a second straight championship. Here, Zito scores Brazil's second goal, the game-winner.

FIFA GRANTED CHILE THE 1962 WORLD CUP, AS IF IT WERE CONSOLATION for a series of destructive earthquakes that preceded this showcase event. A new stadium was constructed in Santiago, and all might have gone perfectly if not for the sudden overemphasis on defense by nearly all participants and an unfortunate skirmish with the Italians.

Italy had managed to outrage the South Americans by importing several top Brazilian and Argentinian players, and by threatening to sign others. To exacerbate matters, a couple of Italian correspondents reported that conditions in impoverished Chile were quite awful. "Malnutrition, prostitution, illiteracy, alcoholism, wretchedness," wrote Corrado Pizzenelli about the host country. When Chile and Italy were placed, as if by fate, in the same first-round grouping, a confrontation was inevitable.

The Chileans carried their country's grudge onto the field, spitting at the Italian players and calling them unprintable names. Then, Chilean forward Leonel Sanchez—son of a professional boxer—slugged Humbert Maschio and broke his nose. English referee Ken Aston missed this awful foul entirely, and later ejected two Italians for retaliating. Italy, playing with only nine men, had their World Cup hopes dashed 2–0. After such sweet revenge, Chile's elimination by Brazil was almost palatable for the host country.

Fortunately, the rest of the tournament went according to the usual plan: A favorite, Brazil soared through its draw behind the brilliance of Garrincha, Vava, and Pelé (whose reputation was assured with a goal against Mexico, in which he dribbled through no fewer than four defenders); an underdog, Czechoslovakia wound its way into the final with a few low-scoring upsets.

The 4–3–3 formation was now all the rage in Europe, and defensive soccer would rule until Holland demonstrated a much more exhilarating formation in 1974.

The Czechs, technically sound but relatively methodical, scored first in the final on a goal in the sixteenth minute by Josef Masopust. The Brazilians, however, had too many skillful finishers to fritter away all their opportunities in the Czech box. Amarildo, Zito, and Vava all scored for a 3–1 Brazilian championship that confirmed the era's pecking order.

© UPI/Bettmann Newsphotos

Brazil's Amarildo (left) and Chile's Rojas vie for a loose ball during a semifinal match. The loud, partisan home crowd was not enough to offset two goals apiece from Vava and Garrincha. Brazil won, 4–2, en route to the title.

1962 · Chile

GROUP 1

Uruguay (0)2	**Colombia** (0)1		
(Cubilla, Sasia)	(Zaluaga)		
USSR (0)2	**Yugoslavia** (0)0		
(Ivanov, Ponedelnik)			
Yugoslavia (2)3	**Uruguay** (1)1		
(Skoblar, Galic, Jerkovic)	(Cabrera)		
USSR (3)4	**Colombia** (1)4		
(Ivanov 2, Chislenko, Ponedelnik)	(Aceros, Coll, Rada, Klinger)		
USSR (1)2	**Uruguay** (0)1		
(Mamikin, Ivanov)	(Sasia)		
Yugoslavia (2)5	**Colombia** (0)0		
(Galic, Jerkovic 3, Melic)			

	GP	W	D	L	GF	GA	Pts
USSR	3	2	1	0	8	5	5
Yugoslavia	3	2	0	1	8	3	4
Uruguay	3	1	0	2	4	6	2
Colombia	3	0	1	2	5	11	1

GROUP 2

Chile (1)3	**Switzerland** (1)1		
(Sanchez, L. 2, Ramirez)	(Wuthrich)		
German FR (0)0	**Italy** (0)0		
Chile (0)2	**Italy** (0)0		
(Ramirez, Toro)			
German FR (1)2	**Switzerland** (1)1		
(Brulls, Seeler)	(Schneiter)		
German FR (1)2	**Chile** (0)0		
(Szymaniak*, Seeler)			
Italy (1)3	**Switzerland** (0)0		
(Mora, Bulgarelli 2)			

	GP	W	D	L	GF	GA	Pts
German FR	3	2	1	0	4	1	5
Chile	3	2	0	1	5	3	4
Italy	3	1	1	1	3	2	3
Switzerland	3	0	0	3	2	8	0

GROUP 3

Brazil (0)2	**Mexico** (0)0		
(Zagalo, Pele)			
Czech (0)1	**Spain** (0)0		
(Stibranyi)			
Brazil (0)0	**Czech** (0)0		
Spain (0)1	**Mexico** (0)0		
(Peiro)			
Brazil (0)2	**Spain** (1)1		
(Amarildo 2)	(Adelardo)		
Mexico (2)3	**Czech** (1)1		
(Diaz, Del Aguila, Hernandez, H.*)	(Masek)		

	GP	W	D	L	GF	GA	Pts
Brazil	3	2	1	0	4	1	5
Czechoslovakia	3	1	1	1	2	3	3
Mexico	3	1	0	2	3	4	2
Spain	3	1	0	2	2	3	2

GROUP 4

Argentina (1)1	**Bulgaria** (0)0		
(Facundo)			
Hungary (1)2	**England** (0)1		
(Tichy, Albert)	(Flowers*)		
England (2)3	**Argentina** (0)1		
(Flowers,* Charlton, R., Greaves)	(Sanfilippo)		
Hungary (4)6	**Bulgaria** (0)1		
(Albert 3, Tichy 2, Solymosi)	(Sokolov)		
Argentina (0)0	**Hungary** (0)0		
England (0)0	**Bulgaria** (0)0		

	GP	W	D	L	GF	GA	Pts
Hungary	3	2	1	0	8	2	5
England	3	1	1	1	4	3	3
Argentina	3	1	1	1	2	3	3
Bulgaria	3	0	1	2	1	7	1

QUARTERFINALS

Yugoslavia (1)1	**German FR** (0)0		
(Radakovic)			
Brazil (1)3	**England** (1)1		
(Garrincha 2, Vava)	(Hitchens)		
Chile (2)2	**USSR** (1)1		
(Sanchez, L., Rojas)	(Chislenko)		
Czech (1)1	**Hungary** (0)0		
(Scherer)			

SEMIFINALS

Brazil (2)4	**Chile** (1)2		
(Garrincha 2, Vava 2)	(Toro, Sanchez, L.*)		
Czech (0)3	**Yugoslavia** (0)1		
(Kadraba, Scherer 2*)	(Jerkovic)		

THIRD PLACE GAME (Santiago)

Chile (0)1	**Yugoslavia** (0)0		
(Rojas)			

FINAL (Santiago, 6/17/62)

Brazil (1)3	**Czech** (1)1		
(Amarildo, Zito, Vava)	(Masopust)		

Brazil: Glymar; Santos, D., Santos, N.; Zito, Mauro, Zozimo; Garrincha, Didi, Vava, Amarildo, Zagalo

Czechoslovakia: Schroiff; Tichy, Novak, Pluskal, Popluhar, Masopust; Pospichal, Scherer, Kvasnak, Kadraba, Jelinek

Referee: Latychev (USSR)

*Penalty kick goal

WORLD CUP VIII: *ENGLAND, 1966*

FINALLY, AFTER THIRTY-TWO YEARS, GLORY AGAIN VISITED THE HOME side. It found the time, also, to anoint the oddest quarterfinalists in World Cup history.

England's mentor Alf Ramsey had embraced the 4–3–3 formation for his bruising, tackling side, and it was a perfect fit. Goaltender Gordon Banks had already established himself as a steady anchor, and with dependable defenders like George Cohen and Ray Wilson, the British defense was next to impregnable. The English were never boring, either—not with the genius of left-half Bobby Moore and Bobby Charlton up front.

While England sputtered a bit early in the tournament, it was defending champion Brazil that faltered terminally. Garrincha was still recovering from a car accident, and Pelé was shadowed, kicked, and eventually sidelined. He was unable to play against Hungary, a match Brazil lost 3–1. He played only half-effectively against Portugal, another 3–1 defeat, before he was cruelly undercut by Portuguese defender Morais. Pelé was carried off the field, unprotected once more by World Cup referees.

A much happier story emerged from a most unexpected quarter. The small, quick North Koreans, lightly regarded after beating only Australia to qualify, pulled off the greatest upset since the United States had nipped England sixteen years earlier. In Middlesbrough, before an enthusiastic crowd, the Koreans defeated haughty Italy 1–0. The only goal came late in the first half on a steal, dribble, and sharp crossing shot from inside-left Pak Doo Ik. The Koreans were

The beginning of a more cynical era in soccer. **Above:** *Pelé is badgered, shadowed, tripped (here, by McKinnon of Scotland), and eventually knocked out of the World Cup. Never again would a superstar be permitted to weave his magic without paying a stiff price.* **Right:** *A first-round miracle: North Korea eliminates mighty Italy, 1–0. Here, Barison (Italy) temporarily stems the Koreans' lightning assault with a clearing head ball.*

ENGLAND 3 GERMANY W. 2

© Syndication International, Ltd.

in the quarterfinals; the Italians were out. Worse, this had been no fluke. Back in Italy, the players were mocked for their defeat for nearly a year. The coach, of course, was replaced.

The final at Wembley, televised live even in the usually indifferent United States, was a melodramatic presentation of the first order between England and West Germany. West German coach Helmut Schoen ordered star Franz Beckenbauer to shadow Charlton all day, blunting the Germans' creativity. The English led 2–1 after eighty-nine minutes, but then Lothar Emmerich's free kick caromed off a teammate and back to a German defender, Weber, who scored just before the final whistle. The match went into overtime.

In the single most controversial World Cup goal, Geoff Hurst's shot ten minutes into overtime banged off the crossbar and down onto the goal line. Despite vigorous protests from Germany, the Russian linesman, Bakhramov, ruled the ball had gone over the line for a goal. England led 3–2, and Hurst finished his hat trick (scoring three goals in one game) with a left-footed line drive from just inside the penalty area. England, the host and inventor of this sport, had ridden its 4–3–3 to a 4–2 championship.

Geoff Hurst finishes off his hat trick with England's fourth goal in a 4–2 overtime win over West Germany.

Wolfgang Weber (left) scores Germany's second goal during the last seconds of regulation play in the final against England. Less than an hour later, goalie Gordon Banks (right) would be celebrating an overtime victory and England's first championship.

1966 · England

GROUP 1

England	(0)0	**Uruguay**	(0)0
France	(0)1	**Mexico**	(0)1
(Hausser)		*(Borja)*	
Uruguay	(2)2	**France**	(1)1
(Rocha, Cortex)		*De Bourgoing*)*	
England	(1)2	**Mexico**	(0)0
(Charlton, R., Hunt)			
Uruguay	(0)0	**Mexico**	(0)0
England	(1)2	**France**	(0)0
(Hunt 2)			

	GP	W	D	L	GF	GA	Pts
England	3	2	1	0	4	0	5
Uruguay	3	1	2	0	2	1	4
Mexico	3	0	2	1	1	3	2
France	3	0	1	2	2	5	1

GROUP 2

German FR	(3)5	**Switzerland**	(0)0
(Held, Haller 2*, Beckenbauer 2)			
Argentina	(0)2	**Spain**	(0)1
(Artime 2)		*(Pirri)*	
Spain	(0)2	**Switzerland**	(1)1
(Sanchis, Amancio)		*(Quentin)*	
Argentina	(0)0	**German FR**	(0)0
Argentina	(0)2	**Switzerland**	(0)0
(Artime, Onega)			
German FR	(1)2	**Spain**	(1)1
(Emmerich, Seeler)		*(Fuste)*	

	GP	W	D	L	GF	GA	Pts
German FR	3	2	1	0	7	1	5
Argentina	3	2	1	0	4	1	5
Spain	3	1	0	2	4	5	2
Switzerland	3	0	0	3	1	9	0

GROUP 3

Brazil	(1)2	**Bulgaria**	(0)0
(Pele, Garrincha)			
Portugal	(1)3	**Hungary**	(0)1
(Augusto 2, Torres)		*(Bene)*	
Hungary	(1)3	**Brazil**	(1)1
(Bene, Farkas, Meszoly*)		*(Tostao)*	
Portugal	(2)3	**Bulgaria**	(0)0
(Vutzov, o.g., Eusebio, Torres)			
Portugal	(2)3	**Brazil**	(0)1
(Simoes, Eusebio 2)		*(Rildo)*	
Hungary	(2)3	**Bulgaria**	(1)1
(Davidov, o.g., Meszoly, Bene)		*(Asparoukhov)*	

	GP	W	D	L	GF	GA	Pts
Portugal	3	3	0	0	9	2	6
Hungary	3	2	0	1	7	5	4
Brazil	3	1	0	2	4	6	2
Bulgaria	3	0	0	3	1	8	0

GROUP 4

USSR	(2)3	**Korea DPR**	(0)0
(Malafeev 2, Banischevsky)			
Italy	(1)2	**Chile**	(0)0
(Mazzola, Barison)			
Chile	(1)1	**Korea DPR**	(0)1
(Marcos*)		*(Pak Seung Jin)*	
USSR	(0)1	**Italy**	(0)0
(Chislenko)			
Korea DPR	(1)1	**Italy**	(0)0
(Pak Doo Ik)			
USSR	(1)2	**Chile**	(1)1
(Porkujan 2)		*(Marcos)*	

	GP	W	D	L	GF	GA	Pts
USSR	3	3	0	0	6	1	6
Korea DPR	3	1	1	1	2	4	3
Italy	3	1	0	2	2	2	2
Chile	3	0	1	2	2	5	1

QUARTERFINALS

England	(0)1	**Argentina**	(0)0
(Hurst)			
German FR	(1)4	**Uruguay**	(0)0
(Held, Beckenbauer, Seeler, Haller)			
Portugal	(2)5	**Korea DPR**	(3)3
(Eusebio 4**, Augusto)		*(Pak Seung Jin, Yang Sung Kook, Li Dong Woon)*	
USSR	(1)2	**Hungary**	(0)1
(Chislenko, Porkujan)		*(Bene)*	

SEMIFINALS

German FR	(1)2	**USSR**	(0)1
(Haller, Beckenbauer)		*(Porkujan)*	
England	(1)2	**Portugal**	(0)1
(Charlton, R. 2)		*(Eusebio*)*	

THIRD PLACE GAME *(London)*

Portugal	(1)2	**USSR**	(1)1
(Eusebio*, Torres)		*(Malafeev)*	

FINAL *(London, 7/30/66)*

England	(1)(2)4	**Grmn FR**	(1)(2)2
(Hurst 3, Peters)		*(Haller, Weber)*	

England: Banks; Cohen, Wilson; Stiles, Charlton, J., Moore; Ball, Hurst, Hunt, Charlton, R., Peters

German FR: Tilkowski; Hottges, Schnellinger; Beckenbauer, Schulz, Weber; Held, Haller, Seeler, Overath, Emmerich

Referee: Dienst (Switzerland)

*Penalty kick goal

WORLD CUP IX: MEXICO, 1970

THE CHOICE OF MEXICO AND ITS HIGH-ALTITUDE CITIES OF MEXICO City, Guadalajara, Puebla, and Toluca to host this World Cup proved to be the ultimate crucible for the international cast of soccer stars. They played their matches at altitudes of 7,000 feet (2,133 m), in ninety degree Fahrenheit (thirty-two degree Centigrade) temperatures, with the sun directly overhead to accommodate worldwide television schedules.

At least FIFA had decided to allow substitutions for the first time, which helped. But this World Cup would be a war of attrition, as well as one of skill.

Perhaps more than ever, the South Americans' aggressive, artistic style was becoming differentiated from the European style. Brazil, two-time champs, epitomized their region's wonderful flair. Pelé, now at the height of his game, was supported by such stars as Rivelino, Gerson, Jaairzinho, Tostao, and captain Carlos Alberto. Only the goalie, Felix, appeared suspect. The Europeans, more pedestrian, still fielded three particularly rugged clubs: Italy, Germany, and defending champion England. The English, however, were battling more than just opponents. They had somehow usurped Italy's unfavorite position among Central and South Americans, in part because of a trumped-up charge of jewelry theft lodged against Bobby Moore in Bogota, Colombia. This excess baggage eventually took its toll.

Despite the absence of North Korea, which elected not to play a qualifier against Israel for political reasons, the sixteen-nation draw was not without its fringe entrants. Israel had qualified, as had Morocco. El Salvador earned a spot in the most painful way imaginable. Its victory over Honduras in a Confederation of North and Central American and Caribbean Football Associations (CONCACAF) qualifying match began a short soccer war against its Central American rival, in which three thousand people were killed.

The tragic loss of life, pointless from the start, seemed even more absurd after El Salvador's early elimination. In a match against Mexico, Egyptian referee Hussain Kandil awarded El Salvador a free kick minutes before halftime. Instead, the Mexicans took the kick, scoring a goal against the startled Salvadorans. The Salvadorean players argued, cried, and staged a sit-in on the field, all in

Exhausted English players prepare for overtime, again, in the quarterfinal against Germany. This time, Gerd Muller would reverse their fortunes.

© Syndication International, Ltd

vain. The bizarre goal counted—not many refs would disallow a host team's goal in the World Cup—and Mexico went on to win 4–0.

Brazil, not surprisingly, steamrolled its way to the final with a 3–1 win over Uruguay, and met the high-scoring Italian team in Mexico City. The Italians, now fully recovered from their North Korean fiasco, were led on the attack by veterans Luigi Riva and Gianni Rivera, who had been unthinkingly benched at the start of the tournament. Both teams had won two World Cups, and the winner would retire the Jules Rimet trophy permanently. (If any team wins the World Cup three times, they then take the trophy, which is replaced and renamed.)

This, however, would be a World Cup won not by a nation, but by a single man. Pelé, in full brilliance, scored a spectacular header and set up two other goals in a 4–1 Brazil victory. This was Pelé's last World Cup appearance and, not coincidentally, Brazil's last championship for quite a while.

Opposite page: Pelé weaves World Cup magic one last time, leading Brazil to a 4–1 victory over Italy in the final at Mexico City. Who could replace him?

THIS WOULD BE A WORLD CUP WON NOT BY A NATION, BUT BY A SINGLE MAN, PELÉ.

1970 · Mexico

GROUP 1

Mexico	(0)0	USSR		(0)0
Belgium	(1)3	El Salvador		(0)0
(Van Moer 2, Lambert*)				
USSR	(1)4	Belgium		(0)1
(Byshovets 2, Asatiani, Khmelnitsky)		*(Lambert)*		
Mexico	(1)4	El Salvador		(0)0
(Valdivia 2, Fragoso, Basaguren)				
USSR	(0)2	El Salvador		(0)0
(Byshovets 2)				
Mexico	(1)1	Belgium		(0)0
(Pena*)				

	GP	W	D	L	GF	GA	Pts
USSR	3	2	1	0	6	1	5
Mexico	3	2	1	0	5	0	5
Belgium	3	1	0	2	4	5	2
El Salvador	3	0	0	3	0	9	0

GROUP 2

Uruguay	(1)2	Israel		(0)0
(Maneiro, Mujica)				
Italy	(1)1	Sweden		(0)0
(Domenghini)				
Uruguay	(0)0	Italy		(0)0
Sweden	(0)1	Israel		(0)1
(Turesson)		*(Spiegler)*		
Sweden	(0)1	Uruguay		(0)0
(Grahn)				
Italy	(0)0	Israel		(0)0

	GP	W	D	L	GF	GA	Pts
Italy	3	1	2	0	1	0	4
Uruguay	3	1	1	1	2	1	3
Sweden	3	1	1	1	2	2	3
Israel	3	0	2	1	1	3	2

GROUP 3

England	(0)1	Romania		(0)0
(Hurst)				
Brazil	(1)4	Czech		(1)1
(Rivelino, Pele, Jairzinho 2)		*(Petras)*		
Romania	(0)2	Czech		(1)1
(Neagu, Dumitrache)		*(Petras)*		
Brazil	(0)1	England		(0)0
(Jairzinho)				
Brazil	(2)3	Romania		(0)2
(Pele 2, Jairzinho)		*(Dumitrache, Dembrovski)*		
England	(0)1	Czech		(0)0
(Clarke*)				

	GP	W	D	L	GF	GA	Pts
Brazil	3	3	0	0	8	3	6
England	3	2	0	1	2	1	4
Romania	3	1	0	2	4	5	2
Czechoslovakia	3	0	0	3	2	7	0

GROUP 4

Peru	(0)3	Bulgaria		(1)2
(Gallardo, Chumpitaz, Cubillas)		*(Dermendjiev, Bonev)*		
German FR	(0)2	Morocco		(1)1
(Seeler, Muller)		*(Houmane)*		
Peru	(0)3	Morocco		(0)0
(Cubillas 2, Challe)				
German FR	(2)5	Bulgaria		(1)2
(Libuda, Muller 3, Seeler)		*(Nikodimov, Kolev)*		
German FR	(3)3	Peru		(1)1
(Muller 3)		*(Cubillas)*		
Bulgaria	(1)1	Morocco		(0)1
(Jetchev)		*(Gazouani)*		

	GP	W	D	L	GF	GA	Pts
German FR	3	3	0	0	10	4	6
Peru	3	2	0	1	7	5	4
Bulgaria	3	0	1	2	5	9	1
Morocco	3	0	1	2	2	6	1

QUARTERFINALS

Uruguay	(0)(0)1	USSR		(0)(0)0
(Esparrago)				
Italy	(1)4	Mexico		(1)1
(Domenghini, Riva 2, Rivera)		*(Gonzales)*		
Brazil	(2)4	Peru		(1)2
(Rivelino, Tostao 2, Jairzinho)		*(Gallardo, Cubillas)*		
German FR	(0)(2)3	England	(1)(2)2
(Beckenbauer, Seeler, Muller)		*(Mullery, Peters)*		

SEMIFINALS

Italy	(1)(1)4	German FR		(0)(1)3
(Boninsegna, Burgnich, Riva, Rivera)		*(Schnellinger, Muller 2)*		
Brazil	(1)3	Uruguay		(1)1
(Clodoaldo, Jairzinho, Rivelino)		*(Cubilla)*		

THIRD PLACE GAME *(Mexico City)*

German FR	(1)1	Uruguay		(0)0
(Overath)				

FINAL *(Mexico City, 6/20/70)*

Brazil	(1)4	Italy		(1)1
(Pele, Gerson, Jairzinho, Carlos Alberto)		*(Boninsegna)*		

Brazil: Feliz; Carlos Alberto, Brito, Wilson, Piazza, Everaldo; Clodoaldo, Gerson; Jairzinho, Tostao, Pele, Rivelino
Italy: Albertosi; Burgnich, Cera, Rosato, Facchetti; Bertini (s. Juliano), Mazzola, De Sisti; Domenghini, Boninsegna (s. Rivera), Riva

Referee: Glockner (East Germany)

*Penalty kick goal

WORLD CUP X: WEST GERMANY, 1974

LIKE A BREATH OF FRESH AIR FROM THE NORTH, HOLLAND PURIFIED the sport of soccer in Europe in the years leading up to this World Cup. The Dutch played a different, less encumbered style than the English, German, and Italian teams that had once dominated with structured "positionalism." Instead, the Netherlands introduced a system called "total soccer," using a core of immensely talented and mobile players from club teams Ajax and Feyenoord.

The Dutch switched positions as they moved upfield on the attack, looking—it always seemed—for their superstar, Johann Cruyff. Cruyff was the top player in Europe and, now that Pelé had retired from the Brazilian national team and was missing from the international scene, in the world. But Holland's dependence on Cruyff's finishing skills would inevitably lead to its downfall, proving the Dutch were not quite as total as advertised.

Because of the aging of the South American teams, it was expected from the start that the final would involve Holland and another European team—possibly host West Germany, with its stable of Bayern Munich stars. That is just the way things turned out, with few surprises until the very end.

Along the way, there were a few diversions. Italian striker Giorgio Chinaglia, a future New York Cosmos star, hit his coach, Feruccio Valcareggi after being pulled from a game. East Germany stacked its defense eight-men deep and pulled off a 1–0 upset over rival West Germany (which advanced, anyway, into the next round). Scottish fans, frustrated by their team's scoreless tie with Brazil, sacked the city of Frankfurt on a one-night rampage. The Scots were eventually eliminated without losing a single match on goal differential (the number of goals scored by the team minus the number of goals scored against the team).

Holland v. Argentina. Cruyff goes past Carnovali to score in this 1974 World Cup match.

© Syndication International, Ltd.

West German hero Sepp Maier, the inspired goalie who stopped Holland and Johann Cruyff with a 2–1 score.

After West Germany nipped Poland 1–0, and the Netherlands romped past such traditional powers as Argentina, East Germany, and Brazil (by an aggregate score of 8–0), the final was set for Munich. It seemed nobody would stop Cruyff and his attacking partners, Johan Neeskins, Johnny Rep, Rob Resenbrink, and Wim Van Hanegem.

Holland struck first, just ninety seconds into the match, when Cruyff drove into the penalty area and was roughly tackled for a penalty kick. But Berti Vogts was assigned to shadow Cruyff wherever he roamed, and somehow the Dutch could not solve this relatively simple defensive ploy. Paul Breitner equalized the score in the twenty-sixth minute on a penalty kick, and Gerd Muller scored the winner, a sloppy boot, early in the second half. Holland, classy to the end, attacked willfully, almost spiritually. But Cruyff could not shake Vogts, and German goalie Sepp Maier turned back shots from Rep and the others.

In the end, Holland would have to settle for runner-up, as Hungary did twenty years earlier. It was a humbling experience, but most fans still understood it was the Dutch who had revitalized the game in Europe, not the dogged West Germans.

1974 · West Germany

GROUP 1

German FR (1)1 **Chile** (0)0
(Breitner)

German DR (0)2 **Australia** (0)0
(Curran, o.g.,
  Streich)

German FR (2)3 **Australia** (0)0
(Overath,
  Cullmann,
  Muller)

Chile (0)1 **German DR** (0)1
(Ahumada) (Hoffman)

Australia (0)0 **Chile** (0)0

German DR (0)1 **German FR** (0)0
(Sparwasser)

	GP	W	D	L	GF	GA	Pts
German DR	3	2	1	0	4	1	5
German FR	3	2	0	1	4	1	4
Chile	3	0	2	1	1	2	2
Australia	3	0	1	2	0	5	1

GROUP 2

Brazil (0)0 **Yugoslavia** (0)0

Scotland (2)2 **Zaire** (0)0
(Lorimar, Jordan)

Yugoslavia (6)9 **Zaire** (0)0
(Bajevic 3, Djazic,
  Surjek,
  Katalinski,
  Bogicevic,
  Oblak, Petkovic)

Scotland (0)0 **Brazil** (0)0

Brazil (1)3 **Zaire** (0)0
(Jairzinho,
  Rivelino,
  Valdomiro)

Scotland (0)1 **Yugoslavia** (0)1
(Jordan) (Karasi)

	GP	W	D	L	GF	GA	Pts
Yugoslavia	3	1	2	0	10	1	4
Brazil	3	1	2	0	3	0	4
Scotland	3	1	2	0	3	1	4
Zaire	3	0	0	3	0	14	0

GROUP 3

Sweden (0)0 **Bulgaria** (0)0

Netherlands (1)2 **Uruguay** (0)0
(Rep 2)

Netherlands (0)0 **Sweden** (0)0

Bulgaria (0)1 **Uruguay** (0)1
(Bonev) (Pavoni)

Sweden (0)3 **Uruguay** (0)0
(Edstroem 2,
  Sandberg)

Netherlands (2)4 **Bulgaria** (0)1
(Neeskens 2**, (Krol, o.g.)
  Rep, de Jong)

	GP	W	D	L	GF	GA	Pts
Netherlands	3	2	1	0	6	1	5
Sweden	3	1	2	0	3	0	4
Bulgaria	3	0	2	1	2	5	2
Uruguay	3	0	1	2	1	6	1

GROUP 4

Italy (0)3 **Haiti** (0)1
(Rivera, Benetti, (Sanon)
  Anastasi)

Poland (2)3 **Argentina** (0)2
(Lato 2, (Heredia,
  Szarmach) Babington)

Poland (5)7 **Haiti** (0)0
(Lato 2, Deyna,
  Szarmach 3, Gorgon)

Argentina (1)1 **Italy** (1)1
(Houseman) (Perfumo, o.g.)

Argentina (2)4 **Haiti** (0)1
(Yazalde 2, (Sanon)
  Houseman, Ayala)

Poland (2)2 **Italy** (0)1
(Szarmach, Deyna) (Capello)

	GP	W	D	L	GF	GA	Pts
Poland	3	3	0	0	12	3	6
Argentina	3	1	1	1	7	5	3
Italy	3	1	1	1	5	4	3
Haiti	3	0	0	3	2	14	0

GROUP A (SECOND ROUND)

Netherlands (2)4 **Argentina** (0)0
(Cruyff 2, Rep, Krol)

Brazil (0)1 **German DR** (0)0
(Rivelino)

Netherlands (1)2 **German DR** (0)0
(Neeskens,
  Resenbrink)

Brazil (1)2 **Argentina** (1)1
(Rivelino, Jairzinho) (Brindisi)

Netherlands (0)2 **Brazil** (0)0
(Neeskens, Cruyff)

Argentina (1)1 **German DR** (1)1
(Houseman) (Streich)

	GP	W	D	L	GF	GA	Pts
Netherlands	3	3	0	0	8	0	6
Brazil	3	2	0	1	3	3	4
German DR	3	0	1	2	1	4	1
Argentina	3	0	1	2	2	7	1

GROUP B

German FR (0)2 **Yugoslavia** (0)0
(Breitner, Müller)

Poland (1)1 **Sweden** (0)0
(Lato)

Poland (1)2 **Yugoslavia** (1)1
(Denya*, Lato) (Karasi)

German FR (0)4 **Sweden** (1)2
(Overath, Bonhof, (Edstroem,
  Grabowski, Sandberg)
  Hoeness*)

German FR (0)1 **Poland** (0)0
(Müller)

Sweden (1)2 **Yugoslavia** (1)1
(Edstroem, (Surjek)
  Torstensson)

	GP	W	D	L	GF	GA	Pts
German FR	3	3	0	0	7	2	6
Poland	3	2	0	1	3	2	4
Sweden	3	1	0	2	4	6	2
Yugoslavia	3	0	0	3	2	6	0

THIRD PLACE GAME (Munich)

Poland (0)1 **Brazil** (0)0
(Lato)

FINAL (Munich, 7/7/74)

German FR (2)2 **Netherlands** (1)1
(Breitner*, Muller) (Neeskens*)

German FR: Maier; Vogts, Beckenbauer,
Schwarzenbeck, Breitner; Hoeness,
Bonhof, Overath; Grabowski, Müller,
Holzenbein
Netherlands: Jongbloed; Suurbier,
Rijsbergen (s. de Jong), Haan, Krol;
Jansen, Neeskens, van Hanagem;
Rep. Cruyff, Resenbrink
(s. R. van der Kerkhof)

Referee: Taylor (England)

*Penalty kick goal

*Johan Neeskens takes another shot for Holland, and
another scoring chance fails. The Dutch, clearly superior,
had to settle for second, like Hungary twenty years earlier.*

WORLD CUP XI: ARGENTINA, 1978

FROM TOTAL SOCCER TO TOTAL SOCCER MANIA. THE WORLD CUP WAS big business now, made profitable by the billions of dollars, lire, francs, and marks pumped into the sport by television and corporate sponsors.

With this kind of explosion and exposure came increasing pressure on the participants themselves. The 1978 World Cup would be remembered, apart from Argentina's two dramatic last victories, for the intense scrutiny and abuse suffered by its coaches.

Among the coaches second- and third-guessed throughout the tournament was Luis Cesar Menotti of Argentina, nicknamed "El Loco" by fans, who passed over blossoming seventeen-year-old Diego Maradona in his selections. Others under fire included West Germany's Helmut Schoen, whose defending champions were no longer capable of mounting a fluid attack; Brazil's Continho, who tried in vain to bring total soccer to the totally individual Brazilians; and Scotland's Ally MacLeod, who put up with more disdain, even, than his peers.

Celebration: A ticker-tape welcome for the world champion Argentines, who honorably defended their home turf in 1978.

THE 1978 WORLD CUP WOULD BE REMEMBERED, APART FROM ARGENTINA'S TWO DRAMATIC LAST VICTORIES, FOR THE INTENSE SCRUTINY AND ABUSE SUFFERED BY ITS COACHES.

For MacLeod, this World Cup was sheer disaster. Fielding several key players slowed by injuries, Scotland fell hard in its opener to Peru, 3–1. Worse, one player, Willy Johnston, failed a drug test (soccer had truly come of age now) that revealed an amphetamine substance in his system. Johnston was banned from soccer for life, and returned to Scotland. Next came a humiliating 1–1 draw with Iran. Finally, the Scots got their act together to defeat Holland 3–2, only to be eliminated by goal differential. MacLeod was dissected and vilified in his nation's press but, to the credit of the Scottish Federation, he was not replaced.

The format of this World Cup, like the one before it, precluded an actual semifinal. The Netherlands, still a world-class team despite the loss of Cruyff, advanced to the final by winning its second-round group over European competitors Italy, Germany, and Austria. The other group was undecided until the final match, a night meeting between Peru and Argentina, with Argentina needing a near-impossible four-goal victory to advance. In a shameful exhibition, Peru, already eliminated, fell totally apart and offered only token defensive resistance. Argentina won 6–0, eliminating undefeated Brazil, sparking a bitter triangular quarrel among the three South American nations that would not cool for some time.

Hard-luck Scotland finally wins one: a 3–2 victory over quadrennial power Holland. Here, Kenny Dalglish beats Jan Jongbloed for Scotland's first goal. The Scots failed to advance to the second round, victims of goal differential.

Left: *On a goal by Mario Kempes, Argentina goes ahead, 2–1, in overtime of the World Cup final against Holland.*
Below: *The agony of defeat.*

Holland, again the superior team on paper and on the field, nearly broke a 1–1 tie in regulation on a shot by Rob Resinbrink that went off a post. Instead, Argentinian striker Kempes scored his second goal of the game in overtime, and Bertoni sealed matters for a 3–1 win. Holland, easily the best team over a five-year period ending in 1978, lost again to another over-achieving host country. And by 1982, this special, talented group would be too old to win a World Cup.

1978 · Argentina

GROUP 1

Italy (1)**2**		**France**		(1)**1**
(Rossi, Zaccarelli)		(Lacombe)		
Argentina (1)**2**		**Hungary**		(1)**1**
(Luque, Bertoni)		(Csapo)		
Italy (2)**3**		**Hungary**		(0)**1**
(Rossi, Bettega, Benetti)		(Toth, A.)		
Argentina (1)**2**		**France**		(0)**1**
(Passarella, Luque)		(Platini)		
France (3)**3**		**Hungary**		(1)**1**
(Lopez, Berdoll, Rocheteau)		(Zombori)		
Italy (0)**1**		**Argentina**		(0)**0**
(Bettega)				

	GP	W	D	L	GF	GA	Pts
Italy	3	3	0	0	6	2	6
Argentina	3	2	0	1	4	3	4
France	3	1	0	2	5	5	2
Hungary	3	0	0	3	3	8	0

GROUP 2

German FR (0)**0**		**Poland**		(0)**0**
Tunisia (0)**3**		**Mexico**		(1)**1**
(Kaabi, Ghommidh, Dhouib)		(Vasquez Ayala)		
German FR (4)**6**		**Mexico**		(0)**0**
(D. Muller, H. Muller, Rummenigge 2, Flohe 2)				
Poland (1)**1**		**Tunisia**		(0)**0**
(Lato)				
Poland (1)**3**		**Mexico**		(0)**1**
(Boniek 2, Deyna)		(Rangel)		
Tunisia (0)**0**		**German FR**		(0)**0**

	GP	W	D	L	GF	GA	Pts
Poland	3	2	1	0	4	1	5
German FR	3	1	2	0	6	0	4
Tunisia	3	1	1	1	3	2	3
Mexico	3	0	0	3	2	12	0

GROUP 3

Austria (1)**2**		**Spain**		(1)**1**
(Schachner, Krankl)		(Dani)		
Sweden (1)**1**		**Brazil**		(1)**1**
(Sjoberg)		(Reinaldo)		
Brazil (0)**0**		**Spain**		(0)**0**
Austria (1)**1**		**Sweden**		(0)**0**
(Krankl)				
Spain (0)**1**		**Sweden**		(0)**0**
(Asensi)				
Brazil (1)**1**		**Austria**		(0)**0**
(Roberto)				

	GP	W	D	L	GF	GA	Pts
Austria	3	2	0	1	3	2	4
Brazil	3	1	2	0	2	1	4
Spain	3	1	1	1	2	2	3
Sweden	3	0	1	2	1	3	1

GROUP 4

Peru (1)**3**		**Scotland**		(1)**1**
(Cueto, Cubillas 2)		(Jordan)		
Netherlands (1)**3**		**Iran**		(0)**0**
(Rensenbrink 3)				
Scotland (1)**1**		**Iran**		(1)**1**
(Eskandarian, o.g.)		(Rowshan)		
Netherlands (0)**0**		**Peru**		(0)**0**
Peru (3)**4**		**Iran**		(1)**1**
(Velasquez, Cubillas 3)		(Rowshan)		
Scotland (1)**3**		**Netherlands**		(1)**2**
(Dalglish, Gemmill 2)		(Rensenbrink, Rep)		

	GP	W	D	L	GF	GA	Pts
Peru	3	2	1	0	7	2	5
Netherlands	3	1	1	1	5	3	3
Scotland	3	1	1	1	5	6	3
Iran	3	0	1	2	2	8	1

GROUP A (SECOND ROUND)

German FR (0)**0**		**Italy**		(0)**0**
Netherlands (3)**5**		**Austria**		(0)**1**
(Brandts, Rensenbrink, Rep 2, W. van der Kerkhof)		(Obermayer)		
Italy (1)**1**		**Austria**		(0)**0**
(Rossi)				
Netherlands (1)**2**		**German FR**		(1)**2**
(Haan, R. van der Kerkhof)		(Abramczik, D. Muller)		
Netherlands (0)**2**		**Italy**		(1)**1**
(Brandts, Haan)		(Brandts, o.g.)		
Austria (0)**3**		**German Fr**		(1)**2**
(Vogts, o.g., Krankl 2)		(Rummenigge, Holzenbein)		

	GP	W	D	L	GF	GA	Pts
Netherlands	3	2	1	0	9	4	5
Italy	3	1	1	1	2	2	3
German FR	3	1	0	2	4	8	2
Austria	3	1	0	2	4	8	2

GROUP B

Argentina (1)**2**		**Poland**		(0)**0**
(Kempes 2)				
Brazil (2)**3**		**Peru**		(0)**0**
(Dirceu 2, Zico)				
Argentina (0)**0**		**Brazil**		(0)**0**
Poland (0)**1**		**Peru**		(0)**0**
(Szarmach)				
Brazil (1)**3**		**Poland**		(1)**1**
(Nelinho, Roberto 2)		(Lato)		
Argentina (2)**6**		**Peru**		(0)**0**
(Kempes 2, Tarantini, Luque 2, Houseman)				

	GP	W	D	L	GF	GA	Pts
Argentina	3	2	1	0	8	0	5
Brazil	3	2	1	0	6	1	5
Poland	3	1	0	2	2	5	2
Peru	3	0	0	3	0	10	0

THIRD PLACE GAME

Brazil (0)**2**		**Italy**		(1)**1**
(Nelinho, Dirceu)		(Causio)		

FINAL (Buenos Aires, 6/25/78)

Argentina (1)**3**		**Netherlands**		**1**
(Kempes 2, Bertoni)		(Nanninga)		

Argentina: Fillol; Olguin, Galvan, Passarella, Tarantini; Ardiles (s. Larrosa). Gallego, Kempes; Bertoni, Luque, Ortiz (s. Houseman)

Netherlands: Jongbloed; Jansen (s. Suurbier). Krol, Brandts, Poortvliet; Neeskens, Haan, W. van der Kerkhof; R. van der Kerkhof. Rep (s. Nanninga), Rensenbrink

Referee: Gonella (Italy)

WORLD CUP XII: SPAIN, 1982

Above: Abdul Aziz Al-Anbari boots the ball for Kuwait in their first-round match against England. The Kuwaitis, offered a $200,000 bonus if they could reach the second round, lost 1–0 to England and never collected. Opposite page: A bad match for Patrick Battiston, and for France, during a 3–1 loss to England. France, however, did recover, rolling to the semifinals.

DR. JOÃO HAVELANGE, PRESIDENT OF FIFA, HAD LONG LOBBIED—against vigorous establishment opposition—to increase the number of competing World Cup nations from sixteen to twenty-four. This would create a few more places for deserving European and South American teams, and more importantly, secure a few berths for developing soccer areas in North America, Asia, and Africa.

In Spain, Havelange's plan prevailed, and soccer's manifest destiny was assured. The newcomers not only acquitted themselves well, they added a great deal of excitement and color to the first round. With the embarrassing exception of Hungary's 10–1 victory over El Salvador, the upstarts were shockingly effective. Cameroon played Peru and Poland to 0–0 ties, then waltzed a dance of death with eventual champion Italy: a 1–1 tie in a desperate game that determined advancement.

Algeria knocked off West Germany 2–1 in a Group 2 match, and upset Chile 3–2. It screamed loud and long when Germany scored a 1–0 "gentlemen's agreement" victory over Austria, a result that allowed both nations to advance and kept Algeria from the second round. Honduras drew with host Spain and with Northern Ireland. Then, there was tiny Kuwait, the small Arab country that did not stop making headlines. Even before the start of the tournament there was news. Kuwait's emir offered the players great riches—$200,000 apiece—if they could advance to the second round; incentive bonuses that were not at all common to this tournament. Kuwait tied favored Czechoslovakia, despite a suspect penalty kick that produced the only Czech goal. Then, in a terribly awkward incident during a match against France, the Kuwaiti prince ordered his players to stop the game until a controversial goal was disallowed. The Soviet referee eventually gave in to the Kuwaiti demands—he was later fired for this nonsense—and the Kuwait Soccer Federation was fined $11,000. The French won anyway, 4–1, and there were no bonuses for anyone.

Among the powerhouses, there were few surprises. Brazil played the most exciting soccer, as usual, but could not sustain its emotion, eventually falling to Italy 3–2 in the second round. France, another enthralling side, featured a potent attack with Michel Platini, but unluckily lost in the semifinals to West Germany, 4–3, in a penalty kick shootout. In that match, German goalie Harald

"Toni" Schumacher jarred French defender Patrick Battiston with a forearm, breaking his jaw and knocking out several teeth.

The real scene-stealer of World Cup XII turned out to be Italy's striker Paolo Rossi, back from a two-year suspension for staying silent about his knowledge of fixed games. Rossi led all World Cup scorers with six goals, including the first score in Italy's 3–1 victory over Germany in the final—a diving header past goalkeeper Toni Schumacher. The Germans were emotionally exhausted from their shootout win over France. Their star, Karl-Heinz Rummenigge, was playing with a nagging hamstring pull. And, perhaps most decisive, the Germans were not quite as skillful as the Italians overall. As two billion soccer fans watched on television, Italy won its third World Cup, tying Brazil for all-time bragging rights.

Two opposing stars, Germany's Karl-Heinz Rummenigge (left) *and Guiseppe Bergoni of Italy* (right), *contest the ball during the final.*

1982 · Spain

Group 1

Italy	(0)0	Poland	(0)0
Peru	(0)0	Cameroon	(0)0
Italy	(1)1	Peru	(0)1
(Conti)		*(Diaz)*	
Poland	(0)0	Cameroon	(0)0
Poland	(0)5	Peru	(1)1
(Smolarek, Lato, Boniek, Buncol, Wlodzimierz)		*(La Rosa)*	
Italy	(0)1	Cameroon	(0)1
(Graziani)			

	GP	W	D	L	GF	GA	Pts
Poland	3	1	2	0	5	1	4
Italy	3	0	3	0	2	2	3
Cameroon	3	0	3	0	1	1	3
Peru	3	0	2	1	2	6	2

Group 2

Algeria	(0)2	German FR	(0)1
(Madjer, Belloumi)		*(Rummenigge)*	
Austria	(1)1	Chile	(0)0
(Schachner)			
German FR	(1)4	Chile	(0)1
(Rummenigge 3, Reinders)		*(Moscoso)*	
Austria	(0)2	Algeria	(0)0
(Schachner, Krankl)			
Algeria	(3)3	Chile	(0)2
(Assad 2, Bensaoula)			
German FR	(1)1	Austria	(0)0
(Hrubesch)			

	GP	W	D	L	GF	GA	Pts
German FR	3	2	0	1	6	3	4
Austria	3	2	0	1	3	1	4
Algeria	3	2	0	1	5	5	4
Chile	3	0	0	3	3	8	0

Group 3

Belgium	(0)1	Argentina	(0)0
(Vandenbergh)			
Hungary	(3)10	El Salvador	(0)1
(Kiss 3, Nyilasi 2, Fazekas 2, Poloskei, Toth, Szentes)		*(Zapata)*	
Argentina	(2)4	Hungary	(0)1
(Maradona 2, Bertoni, Ardiles)		*(Poloskei)*	
Belgium	(1)1	El Salvador	(0)0
(Coeck)			
Belgium	(1)1	Hungary	(0)1
(Czerniatynski)		*(Varga)*	
Argentina	(1)2	El Salvador	(0)0
(Passarella, Bertoni)			

	GP	W	D	L	GF	GA	Pts
Belgium	3	2	1	0	3	1	5
Argentina	3	2	0	1	6	2	4
Hungary	3	1	1	1	12	6	3
El Salvador	3	0	0	3	1	13	0

Group 4

England	(1)3	France	(1)1
(Robson 2, Mariner)		*(Soler)*	
Czech	(1)1	Kuwait	(0)1
(Panenka*)		*(Al-Dakhil)*	
England	(0)2	Czech	(0)0
(Francis, Barmos, o.g.)			

France	(2)4	Kuwait	(0)1
(Platini, Six, Genghini, Bossis)		*(Buloushi)*	
France	(0)1	Czech	(1)1
England	(1)1	Kuwait	(0)0
(Trevor)			

	GP	W	D	L	GF	GA	Pts
England	3	3	0	0	6	1	6
France	3	1	1	1	6	5	3
Czechoslovakia	3	0	2	1	2	4	2
Kuwait	3	0	1	2	2	6	1

Group 5

Honduras	(1)1	Spain	(0)1
(Zelaya)		*(Ufarte*)*	
Yugoslavia	(0)0	N Ireland	(0)0
Spain	(1)2	Yugoslavia	(1)1
(Gomez*, Saura)		*(Gudelj)*	
N Ireland	(1)1	Honduras	(0)1
(Armstrong)		*(Laing)*	
Yugoslavia	(0)1	Honduras	(0)0
(Petrovic*)			
Spain	(0)0	N Ireland	(0)0

	GP	W	D	L	GF	GA	Pts
Spain	3	1	2	0	3	2	4
N Ireland	3	0	3	0	1	1	3
Yugoslavia	3	1	1	1	2	2	3
Honduras	3	0	2	1	2	3	2

Group 6

Brazil	(0)2	USSR	(1)1
(Socrates, Eder)		*(Bal)*	
Scotland	(3)5	New Zealand	(0)2
(Wark 2, Dalglish, Robertson, Archibald)		*(Sumner, Wooddin)*	
Brazil	(1)4	Scotland	(1)1
(Zico, Oscar, Eder, Falcao)		*(Narey)*	
USSR	(1)3	New Zealand	(0)0
(Gavrilov, Blokhin, Baltacha)			
Scotland	(1)2	USSR	(2)2
(Jordan, Souness)		*(Chivadze, Shengelia)*	
Brazil	(2)4	New Zealand	(0)0
(Zico 2, Falcao, Serginho)			

	GP	W	D	L	GF	GA	Pts
Brazil	3	3	0	0	10	2	6
USSR	3	1	1	1	6	4	3
Scotland	3	1	1	1	8	8	3
New Zealand	3	0	0	3	2	12	0

Group A (Second Round)

Poland	(2)3	Belgium	(0)0
(Boniek 3)			
USSR	(0)1	Belgium	(0)0
(Organesyan)			
Poland	(0)0	USSR	(0)0

	GP	W	D	L	GF	GA	Pts
Poland	2	1	1	0	3	0	3
USSR	2	1	1	0	1	0	3
Belgium	2	0	0	2	0	4	0

Group B

German FR	(0)0	England	(0)0

German FR	(0)2	Spain	(0)1
(Littbarski, Fischer)		*(Zamora)*	
England	(0)0	Spain	(0)0

	GP	W	D	L	GF	GA	Pts
Germany	2	1	1	0	2	1	3
England	2	0	2	0	0	0	2
Spain	2	0	1	1	1	2	1

Group C

Italy	(0)2	Argentina	(0)1
(Tardelli, Cabrini)		*(Passarella)*	
Brazil	(1)3	Argentina	(0)1
(Zico, Serginho, Junior)		*(Diaz)*	
Italy	(2)3	Brazil	(1)2
(Rossi 3)		*(Socrates, Falcao)*	

	GP	W	D	L	GF	GA	Pts
Italy	2	2	0	0	5	3	4
Brazil	2	1	0	1	5	4	2
Argentina	2	0	0	2	2	5	0

Group D

France	(1)1	Austria	(0)0
(Genghini)			
N Ireland	(1)2	Austria	(0)2
(Hamilton 2)		*(Pezzey, Hintermaier)*	
France	(1)4	N Ireland	(0)1
(Giresse 2, Rocheteau 2)		*(Armstrong)*	

	GP	W	D	L	GF	GA	Pts
France	2	2	0	0	5	1	4
Austria	2	0	1	1	2	3	1
N Ireland	2	0	1	1	3	6	1

Semifinals

Italy	(1)2	Poland	(0)0
(Rossi 2)			
German FR	(1)(3)4	France	(1)(3)3
(Littbarski, Rummenigge, Fischer, Hrubesch†)		*(Platini, Tresor, Giresse)*	

†*Kicked the deciding penalty shot*

In The Shootout:

German FR	(5)5	France	(4)4
(Littbarski, Kaltz, Breitner, Rummenigge, Hrubesch)		*(Giresse, Amoros, Rocheteau, Platini)*	

Third Place Game

Poland	(2)3	France	(1)2
(Szarmach, Majewski, Kupcewicz)		*(Girard, Couriol)*	

Final *(Madrid, 7/11/82)*

Italy	(0)3	German FR	(0)1
(Rossi, Tardelli, Altobelli)		*(Breitner)*	

Italy: Zoff; Bergomi, Scirea, Collovati, Cabrini; Oriali, Gentile, Tardelli; Conti, Rossi, Graziani (Altobelli, Causio)

German FR: Schumacher; Kaltz, Stielike, K. Foerster, B. Foerster; Dremmler (Hrubesch), Breitner, Briegel; Rummenigge (Mueller), Fischer, Littbarski)

Referee: Coelho (Brazil)

*Penalty kick goal

Paolo Rossi was single-handedly responsible for Italy's second-round win over Brazil in the 1982 World Cup. He scored all three Italian goals in the 3–2 win.

© Vandystadt/Allsport

WORLD CUP XIII: MEXICO, 1986

Mexico, an eleventh-hour substitute as host, tried its best to turn the thirteenth World Cup into a festive occasion. The heat, altitude, and the transportation problems didn't help.

COLOMBIA PULLED OUT AS HOST NATION OF THE THIRTEENTH WORLD Cup at the eleventh hour. With no options west of the Atlantic, the World Cup returned to the heat, and heights, of Mexico in 1986—the first time the tournament was awarded to a country that had already been host. With better preparation by both Mexico and the visitors, the event received more favorable reviews than the 1970 affair and made historic profits. A record attendance of 2.4 million fans watched the matches, and 162 countries followed the television coverage.

Once again with the twenty-four-team format, new blood replenished the old through the early rounds. Morocco became the first African nation to advance into the second round. Upstart Denmark, utilizing a mobile, aggressive set reminiscent of Holland's prior efforts, scored an inspiring 6–1 victory over Uruguay and pulled off an early 2–0 upset over West Germany.

Perhaps most surprising was Belgium, a nation with a bleak soccer history that included a 3–0 defeat to the United States in the 1930 World Cup and a game-fixing scandal within its own pro league in 1982. Things had begun just as ominously in preparation for this World Cup, as Belgium lost to lowly Albania in its first qualifier. But coach Guy Thys watched as his team grew more solid with each match, and Belgium peaked with a 4–3 overtime victory over the Soviet Union and a shootout win over Spain that put it in the semifinals. "Belgium among the four best teams on the planet," wrote *LeSoir,* a leading Belgian newspaper. "Unimaginable, sensational, fabulous!"

Belgium's opponent in the semifinal was Argentina, fortified by the brilliant Diego Maradona, now twenty-five, at the peak of his game. Before the tournament, Maradona had been criticized at home for his physical condition—his stockiness was approaching un-soccer-like dimensions. But here in Mexico he was a blur of efficiency and deadly scoring thrusts. Against England, in a 2–1 quarterfinal victory, Maradona's deceptive moves even fooled Tunisian referee Ali Bennacur. Maradona knocked the ball into the net with his hand on Argentina's first goal, pretending it was a header. Bennacur let it stand.

Maradona scored two spectacular, uncontroversial goals in a 2–0 victory over Belgium (on the second goal, reminiscent of Pelé against Mexico, Maradona dribbled through four defenders), setting up a final against West Germany. The Germans, relying heavily on the goaltending of thirty-two-year-old Toni Schumacher, had knocked out high-flying France 2–0 in the other semifinal.

In the battle of continents, the Germans elected to double-team Maradona with Lothar Matthaeus and anybody else in the near vicinity. Matthaeus fouled Maradona on the right side in the twenty-second minute, and the free kick resulted in a cross and header goal by Jose Luis Brown. Argentina moved ahead 2–0 in the second half on a goal by Jorge Alberto Valdono. But the Germans' vintage star, Karl-Heinz Rummenigge, and Rudi Voeller both

A RECORD ATTENDANCE OF 2.4 MILLION FANS WATCHED THE MATCHES, AND 162 COUNTRIES FOLLOWED THE TELEVISION COVERAGE.

Diego Maradona scores Argentina's first goal in a 2–0 victory over Belgium in the 1986 semifinal.

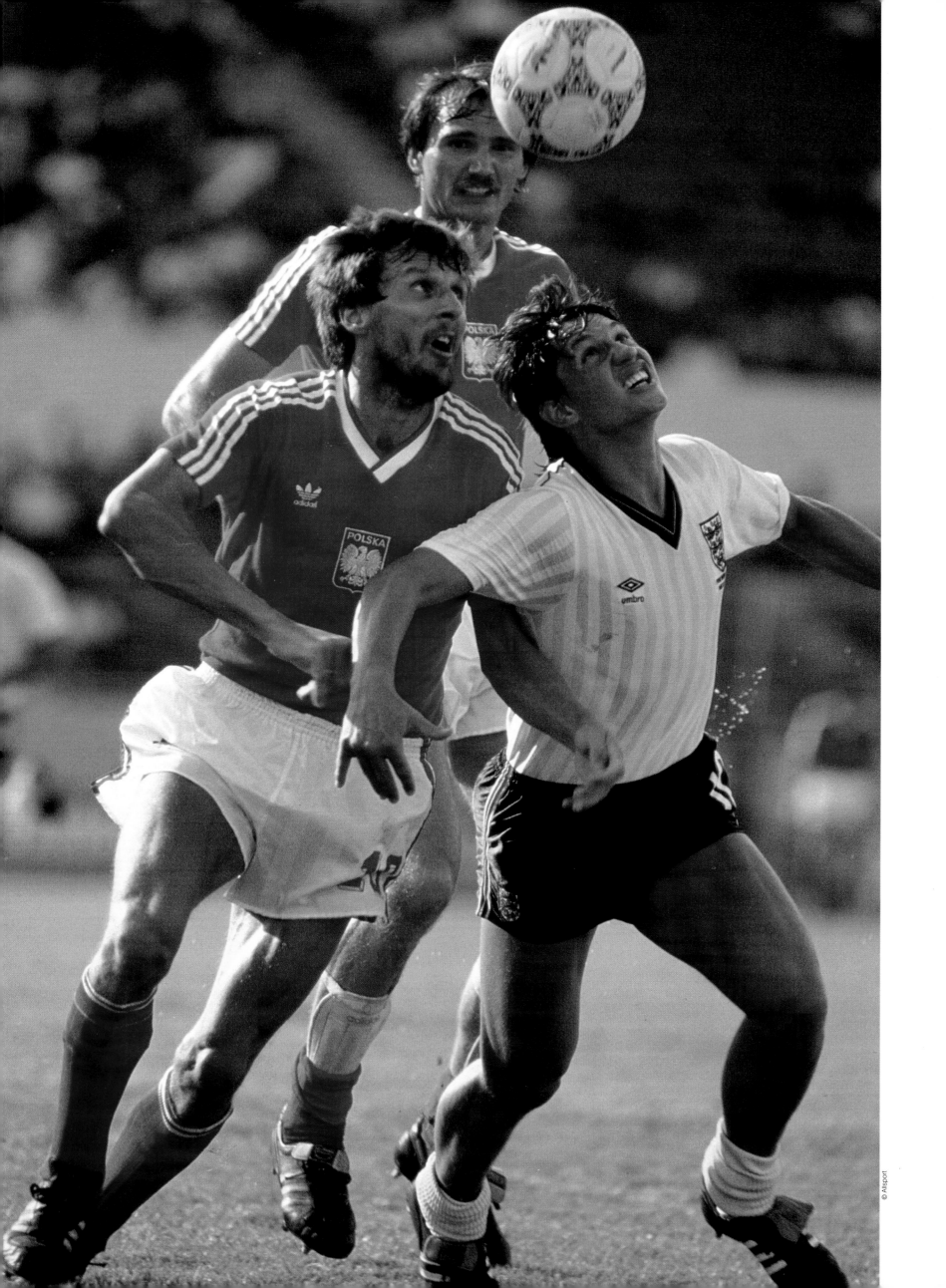

scored to equalize, and it was suddenly anybody's World Cup in the eighty-first minute.

"Our downfall was our happiness after we got the second goal," said Rummenigge, playing his ninety-fifth international match. "I think maybe we figured the game was ours."

Instead, it was Argentina's. The great Maradona led Jorge Burruchaga with a well-timed pass down the right side three minutes after Voeller's score. Burruchaga beat Schumacher from inside the penalty area, and the sea of blue and white Argentinian flags waved proudly for the second time in eight years. As always, no European invader could capture the World Cup in South America.

© David Cannon/Allsport

Opposite page: Gary Lineker (at right), leading goal scorer of the tournament, battles for the ball against Poland. Above: Ditmar Jakobs clears the ball from danger, and from another Argentine threat.

1986 · Mexico

GROUP A

Bulgaria (0)1 **Italy** (1)1
(Sirakov)   (Altobelli)
Argentina (2)3 **South Korea** (0)1
(Valdano 2,   (Chang-Sun Park)
Ruggeri)
Italy (1)1 **Argentina** (1)1
(Altobelli*)   (Maradona)
South Korea (0)1 **Bulgaria** (1)1
(Jong-Boo Kim)   (Getov)
South Korea (0)2 **Italy** (1)3
(Choi, Huh,   (Altobelli 2)
Kwang-Rae Cho
[own goal])
Argentina (1)2 **Bulgaria** (0)0
(Valdano,
Burruchaga)

	GP	W	D	L	GF	GA	Pts
Argentina	3	2	1	0	6	2	5
Italy	3	1	2	0	5	4	4
Bulgaria	3	0	2	1	2	4	2
South Korea	3	0	1	2	4	7	1

GROUP B

Belgium (1)1 **Mexico** (2)2
(Vandenbergh)   (Quirarte,
Sanchez)
Paraguay (1)1 **Iraq** (0)0
(Romero)
Mexico (1)1 **Paraguay** (0)1
(Flores)   (Romero)
Iraq (0)1 **Belgium** (2)2
(Amaiesh)   (Scifo, Claesen*)
Iraq (0)0 **Mexico** (0)1
  (Quirarte)
Paraguay (0)2 **Belgium** (1)2
(Cabanas 2)   (Vercauteren,
Veyt)

	GP	W	D	L	GF	GA	Pts
Mexico	3	2	1	0	4	2	5
Paraguay	3	1	2	0	4	3	4
Belgium	3	1	1	1	5	5	3
Iraq	3	0	0	3	1	4	0

GROUP C

Canada (0)0 **France** (0)1
  (Papin)
Soviet Union (3)6 **Hungary** (0)0
(Yakovenko,
Aleinikov,
Belanov*,
Yaremchuk 2,
Rodionov)
France (0)1 **Soviet Union** (0)1
(Fernandez)   (Rats)
Hungary (1)2 **Canada** (0)0
(Esterhazy, Detari)
Hungary (0)0 **France** (1)3
  (Stopyra, Tigana,
Rocheteau)
Soviet Union (0)2 **Canada** (0)0
(Blokhin, Zavarov)

	GP	W	D	L	GF	GA	Pts
Soviet Union	3	2	1	0	9	1	5
France	3	2	1	0	5	1	5
Hungary	3	1	0	2	2	9	2
Canada	3	0	0	3	0	5	0

GROUP D

Spain (0)0 **Brazil** (0)1
  (Socrates)
Algeria (0)1 **N. Ireland** (1)1
(Zidane)   (Whiteside)
Brazil (0)1 **Algeria** (0)0
(Careca)
N. Ireland (0)1 **Spain** (2)2
(Clarke)   (Butragueno,
Salinas)
N. Ireland (0)0 **Brazil** (2)3
  (Careca 2,
Josimar)
Algeria (0)0 **Spain** (1)3
  (Caldere 2, Eloy)

	GP	W	D	L	GF	GA	Pts
Brazil	3	3	0	0	5	0	6
Spain	3	2	0	1	5	2	4
N. Ireland	3	0	1	2	2	6	1
Algeria	3	0	1	2	1	5	1

GROUP E

Uruguay (1)1 **W. Germany** (0)1
(Alzamendi)   (Allofs)
Scotland (0)0 **Denmark** (0)1
  (Elkjaer)
W. Germany (2)2 **Scotland** (0)1
(Voeller, Allofs)   (Strachan)
Denmark (2)6 **Uruguay** (1)1
(Elkjaer 3, Lerby,   (Francescoli*)
Laudrup, Jesper
Olsen)
Denmark (1)2 **W. Germany** (0)0
(Jesper Olsen*,
Eriksen)
Scotland (0)0 **Uruguay** (0)0

	GP	W	D	L	GF	GA	Pts
Denmark	3	3	0	0	9	1	6
W. Germany	3	1	1	1	3	4	3
Uruguay	3	0	2	1	2	7	2
Scotland	3	0	1	2	1	3	1

GROUP F

Morocco (0)0 **Poland** (0)0
Portugal (0)1 **England** (0)0
(Carlos Manuel)
England (0)0 **Morocco** (0)0
Poland (0)1 **Portugal** (0)0
(Smolarek)
Portugal (0)1 **Morocco** (2)3
(Diamantino)   (Khairi 2,
Abdelkarim
Merry)
England (3)3 **Poland** (0)0
(Lineker 3)

	GP	W	D	L	GF	GA	Pts
Morocco	3	1	2	0	3	1	4
England	3	1	1	1	3	1	3
Poland	3	1	1	1	1	3	3
Portugal	3	1	0	2	2	4	2

SECOND ROUND

Mexico (1)2 **Bulgaria** (0)0
(Negrete, Servin)
Soviet Union (0)3 **Belgium** (1)4
(Belanov 2,   (Scifo, Ceulemans,
Belanov*)   De Mol, Claesen)

Brazil (1)4 **Poland** (0)0
(Socrates*,
Josimar,
Edinho, Careca*)
Argentina (1)1 **Uruguay** (0)0
(Pasculli)
Italy (0)0 **France** (1)2
  (Platini, Stopyra)
Morocco (0)0 **W. Germany** (0)1
  (Matthaus)
England (1)3 **Paraguay** (0)0
(Lineker 2,
Beardsley)
Denmark (1)1 **Spain** (1)5
(Jesper Olsen*)   (Butragueno 3,
Butragueno*,
Goicoechea*)

QUARTERFINALS

Brazil (1)1 **France** (1)1
(Careca)   (Platini)
[France won 4:3   (Stopyra,
on penalties after   Amoros,
extra time]   Bellone,
(Alemao, Zico,   Fernandez)
Branco)
W. Germany (0)0 **Mexico** (0)0
[W. Germany won   (Negrete)
4:1 on penalties
after extra time]
(Allofs, Brehme,
Matthaus, Littbarski)
Argentina (0)2 **England** (0)1
(Maradona 2)   (Lineker)
Spain (0)1 **Belgium** (1)1
(Ceulemans)   (Senor)
[Belgium won 5:4   (Claesen, Scifo,
on penalties after   Broos, Vervoort,
extra time]   Leo van der Elst)
(Senor, Chendo,
Butragueno,
Victor)

SEMIFINAL

France (0)(0)0 **W. Germ.** (1)(1)2
  (Brehme, Voller)
Argentina (0)(2)2 **Belgium** (0)(0)0
(Maradona, 2)

THIRD PLACE GAME (Pfaff)

France (2)4 **Belgium** (1)2
(Ferreri, Papin,   (Ceulemans,
Genghini,   Claesen)
Amoros*)

FINAL (Mexico City, 6/29/86)

W. Germany (0)2 **Argentina** (1)3
(Rummenigge,   (Brown, Valdano,
Voller)   Burruchaga)

West Germany: Schumacher—Jakobs—Forster, Eder—Brehme, Matthaus, Berthold, Magath (62 Hoeness), Briegel—Rummenigge, Allofs (46 Voller)

Argentina: Pumpido—Brown—Cuciuffo, Ruggeri, Olarticoechea—Bastista, Giusti, Burruchaga (90 Trobbiani), Enrique, Maradona—Valdano

Referee: Filho (Brazil)

*Penalty kick goal

WORLD CUP XIV: ITALY, 1990

Air Ireland: Niall Quinn and Tonyca Scarino go flying in a second-round match pitting Ireland against Romania. Ireland won in a penalty-kick shootout, 5–4.

BEFORE WORLD CUP 1990 BEGAN, FIFA PRESIDENT JOÃO HAVELANGE issued directives to referees that he felt would cure what had been ailing world soccer in recent years. Under the doctrine of "Fair Play, Please," Havelange ordered officials to send off any defender hacking down an attacker on a breakaway, and to issue caution cards for virtually all destructive fouls.

In this way, Havelange hoped to reverse the trend toward lower-scoring matches and to open the playing field a bit for the electric stars of the sport. Unfortunately, quite the contrary occurred. Matches at the 1990 World Cup produced a record-low 2.2 goal-per-game average. They were marred by endless penalty kicks, shorthanded situations, and fraudulent claims of injuries.

Festivities started on a high note, although there were early signs of trouble in Cameroon's stunning 1–0 opening game victory over defending champion Argentina on June 8 in Milan. The Indomitable Lions shadowed Diego Maradona closely—Benjamin Massing even watched him tie his shoelaces for several amusing moments—through a scoreless sixty minutes. Then, referee Michel Vautrot of France ejected Kana Biyik for a single tackle, and Cameroon played ten men on eleven. Surprisingly, the African side was energized. Omam Biyik scored a goal against goalie Nery Pumpido in the sixty-seventh minute, and Cameroon held on even after Massing himself was ejected with only two minutes left in the match.

Argentina clearly was punchless, and other supposed powers also lacked teeth up front. Holland, allegedly loaded with attacking strength, managed only three goals in four matches and was eliminated by West Germany in the second round. Brazil, suddenly conservative, managed just four goals in four games and fell to Argentina on a single Maradona dash, also in the second round. Austria's striker Toni Polster, hyped to the heavens as the next great World Cup goal scorer, was shut out as his team was eliminated from Group A competition. The Soviet Union was beaten by Romania, cheated by Maradona, and eliminated far earlier than anybody thought possible.

There were some pleasant surprises, along with the duds. Costa Rica, in its World Cup debut, advanced by defeating both Scotland and Sweden. Romania, some of its fans seeking political asylum outside the stadium, finished ahead of Argentina in volatile

© David Cannon/Allsport

Group B. Czechoslovakia, its giant attackers always a threat on head balls, scored five goals against the woeful Americans, and four against Costa Rica to earn a spot in the quarterfinals. Ireland, a team recruited and trained by Jack Charlton in a disruptive high-ball style, advanced to the quarterfinals with a shootout victory over Romania.

Most amazing and refreshing was Cameroon and its lively reserve, Roger Milla. By advancing to the quarterfinals and refusing to sit on a 2-1 lead over England, Cameroon delighted everybody even in their eventual defeat. Havelange issued some condescending praise for African soccer, but also a very real extra berth for the continent in the 1994 World Cup.

After a while, the shootouts became something of an embarrassment to FIFA, and to soccer. There were four of them in all, two in the semifinals. First, superior Italy, the passionate home team, went down to Argentina in Naples. It seemed impossible, because Italy led early on a rebound goal by Salvatore Schillaci in the seventeenth minute, and had not given up a goal all tournament. But in the sixty-seventh minute, Claudio Caniggia back-headed a cross over goalie Walter Zenga—who was only half-committed to the

A shocker, for openers: Who'd have thought it? Cameroon 1, Argentina 0, kicks off Italia '90 in Milan. Cameroon won with just nine players, but when the dust settled it was Argentina in the final. Here, Omam Biyik scores the only goal of the first match.

Right: Sergio Goycoechea, Argentina's nimble goalie, makes a critical diving save during a shootout against Italy in the semifinals. Argentina won the game, upsetting host Italy, 3–2. Below: Platt of England becomes a German sandwich in a tense semifinal battle in Turin. The match went into another shootout, which Germany won, 4–3.

ball. The match was tied, and Argentina was hoping to hold out for the penalty-kick shootout. Since Schillaci was suffering from a groin pull he was unable to take his turn at the spot and Argentina prevailed in the shootout, 4–3, on some prescient net-minding by Sergio Goycoechea.

This was tragedy, not only for suddenly silent Italy but for soccer. The victorious Argentines had scored but five goals all tournament, and would be no competition at all for England or West Germany. To make matters worse, four of Carlos Bilardo's starters were suspended, three for accumulated yellow cards, another for a red. The blond Caniggia, Argentina's only threat besides Maradona, was one of those out for the final.

The other semifinal was better contested the following night in Turin, but ended in the same random fashion. West Germany led on an indirect free kick by Andreas Brehme in the fifty-ninth minute, and was tied by Gary Lineker in the eightieth minute after a defensive muddle in the box. Another fruitless two periods of overtime followed, and finally the shootout. This time, England free-kick specialists Stuart Pearce and Chris Waddle both failed. Pearce's power shot down the middle bounced off the legs of diving goalkeeper Bodo Illgner. Waddle's shot sailed high. West Germany did not fail once.

The English, whose hooligan fans had turned Italy's cities into armed encampments, deserved better on this night. England had actually outplayed West Germany, looking stronger as the match wore on.

"I say at this level, with this level of importance, you play on with a tie," argued England coach Bobby Robson. "Fitness is part of the fighting spirit. Eventually, someone will crack."

But West German coach Franz Beckenbauer disagreed. He still had a final to play, against the persistent Argentines. During that terrible anticlimactic Sunday in Stadio Olimpico, in Rome, Argentina hung on grimly, booting the ball out of its own end with no direction, hoping only for 120 minutes of scoreless soccer. West

Germany attacked continuously, raining thirty crosses into the box from the wings. But it could not put the ball into the net.

Finally, referee Edgardo Codesal of Mexico intervened, and West Germany was champion. Codesal expelled Argentina defender Pedro Monzon in the sixty-fourth minute, a borderline decision, after Monzon pulled down Juergen Klinsmann on the right wing. In the eighty-fourth minute, Codesal gave West Germany a penalty kick, the end for Argentina. This, too, was debatable, since Roberto Sensini appeared to touch foot to ball before he tackled West German striker Rudi Voeller well to the right of the goal.

Brehme took the penalty, beating Goycoechea low, neatly inside the left-hand post. Finally, Codesal sent off frustrated striker Gustavo Dezotti in the eighty-sixth minute. Dezotti had wrestled down Juergen Kohler by the neck, a cynical way to end a tournament that had gone by the theme, "Fair Play."

"I tried to calm down my players, who at times lose their cool," Argentina's Coach Bilardo said.

At midfield after the match, the Argentines pushed their way unsuccessfully at Codesal. Later, Maradona charged that the Mafia had a hand in the penalty shot against his side. Almost lost in the mess was the fact that the 1990 World Cup, despite all the ugliness, had itself a very deserving champion. West Germany earned its third World Cup with a nice mix of elements; with an attacking

Above: *Diego Maradona is shadowed and neutralized in a dreadful final, won by West Germany, 1–0.*
Below: *Toto Schillaci gets the Argentine treatment from Jose Serrizuela. The Italians, victims of many such harsh tackles, lost heart in the second half and lost the semifinal in a shootout.*

style that used the speed of Klinsmann; the stealth of Voeller; and the planning of midfielder Lothar Matthaeus.

"It's not up to us to choose an adversary," said Beckenbauer, who admitted a match against Italy would have been more aesthetically pleasing. "It's too bad Argentina didn't participate in the game. They were just too weak. They tried to destroy the game. They played a non-game.

"But no team merited this as much as the Germans."

Nearly two billion viewers, and Dr. Havelange, would have had to agree.

Above: *West Germans, soon to be, simply, Germans, celebrate their third World Cup title.* Opposite page: *The West Germans were too quick, even in the air, for the taller Czechs. The Germans won the quarterfinal match, 1–0.*

© Simon Bruty/Allsport

1990 · Italy

GROUP 1

Italy	(0)1	Austria	(0)0
(Schillaci)			
Czchslvkia	(2)5	USA	(0)1
(Skuravy 2, Bilek, Hasek, Luhovy)		(Caligiuri)	
Italy	(1)1	USA	(0)0
(Giannini)			
Czchslvkia	(1)1	Austria	(0)0
(Bilek)			
Italy	(1)2	Czchslvkia	(0)0
(Schillaci, Baggio)			
Austria	(0)2	USA	(0)1
(Ogris, Rodax)		(Murray)	

	GP	W	D	L	GF	GA	Pts
Italy	3	3	0	0	4	0	6
Czechoslovakia	3	2	0	1	6	3	4
Austria	3	1	0	2	2	3	2
USA	3	0	0	3	2	8	0

GROUP 2

Cameroon	(0)1	Argentina	(0)0
(Omam Biyik)			
Romania	(1)2	USSR	(0)0
(Lacatus 2)			
Argentina	(1)2	USSR	(0)0
(Troglio, Burrachaga)			
Cameroon	(0)2	Romania	(0)1
(Milla 2)		(Balint)	
USSR	(2)4	Cameroon	(0)0
(Protassov, Zigmantovich, Zavarov, Dobrovolski)			
Argentina	(0)1	Romania	(0)1
(Monzon)		(Balint)	

	GP	W	D	L	GF	GA	Pts
Cameroon	3	2	0	1	3	4	4
Romania	3	1	1	1	4	3	3
Argentina	3	1	1	1	3	2	3
USSR	3	1	0	2	4	4	2

GROUP 3

Brazil	(1)2	Sweden	(0)1
(Careca 2)		(Brolin)	
Costa Rica	(0)1	Scotland	(0)0
(Cayasso Reid)			
Scotland	(1)2	Sweden	(0)1
(McCall, Johnston)		(Stromberg)	
Brazil	(1)1	Costa Rica	(0)0
(Muller)			
Costa Rica	(0)2	Sweden	(1)1
(Flores Solano, Medford)		(Ekstrom)	
Brazil	(0)1	Scotland	(0)0
(Muller)			

	GP	W	D	L	GF	GA	Pts
Brazil	3	3	0	0	4	1	6
Costa Rica	3	2	0	1	3	2	4
Scotland	3	1	0	2	2	3	2
Sweden	3	0	0	3	3	6	0

GROUP 4

Colombia	(0)2	Un.Ar.Emrts	(0)0
(Redin, Valderrama)			
German FR	(2)4	Yugoslavia	(0)1
(Matthaeus 2, Klinsmann, Voeller)		(Jozic)	
Yugoslavia	(0)1	Colombia	(0)0
(Jozic)			
German FR	(2)5	Un.Ar.Emrts	(0)1
(Voeller 2, Klinsmann, Matthaeus, Bein)		(Mubarak)	
Yugoslavia	(2)4	Un.Ar.Emrts	(1)1
(Susic, Pancev 2, Prosinecki)		(Juma'a)	
German FR	(0)1	Colombia	(0)1
(Littbarski)		(Rincon)	

	GP	W	D	L	GF	GA	Pts
German FR	3	2	1	0	10	3	5
Yugoslavia	3	2	0	1	6	5	4
Colombia	3	1	1	1	3	2	3
Un.Ar.Emrts	3	0	0	3	2	11	0

GROUP 5

Belgium	(0)2	South Korea	(0)0
(De Grijse, De Wolf)			
Uruguay	(0)0	Spain	(0)0
Spain	(1)3	South Korea	(1)1
(Michel 3)		(Hwang Bo Kwang)	
Belgium	(2)3	Uruguay	(0)1
(Clijsters, Scifo, Ceulemans)		(Bengoechea)	
Uruguay	(0)1	South Korea	(0)0
(Fonseca)			
Spain	(2)2	Belgium	(1)1
(Michel, Gorriz)		(Vervoot)	

	GP	W	D	L	GF	GA	Pts
Spain	3	2	1	0	5	2	5
Belgium	3	2	0	1	6	3	4
Uruguay	3	1	1	1	2	3	3
South Korea	3	0	0	3	1	6	0

GROUP 6

England	(1)1	Ireland	(0)1
(Lineker)		(Sheedy)	
Netherlands	(0)1	Egypt	(0)1
(Kieft)		(Abedel Ghani)	
England	(0)0	Netherlands	(0)0
Ireland	(0)0	Egypt	(0)0
Ireland	(0)1	Netherlands	(1)1
(Quinn)		(Gullit)	
England	(0)1	Egypt	(0)0
(Wright)			

	GP	W	D	L	GF	GA	Pts
England	3	1	2	0	2	1	4
Ireland	3	0	3	0	2	2	3
Netherlands	3	0	3	0	2	2	3
Egypt	3	0	2	1	1	2	2

SECOND ROUND

Czchslvkia	(1)4	Costa Rica	(0)1
(Skuhravy 3, Kubik)		(Gonzalez, Brenes)	
Cameroon	(0)(0)2	Columbia	(0)(0)1
(Milla 2)		(Redin)	
German FR	(0)2	Netherlands	(0)1
(Klinsmann, Brehme)		(Koeman)	
Argentina	(0)1	Brazil	(0)0
(Caniggia)			
Ireland	(0)(0)5	Romania	(0)(0)4
Italy	(0)2	Uruguay	(0)0
(Schillaci, Serena)			
England	(0)(0)1	Belgium	(0)(0)0
(Platt)			
Yugslvia	(0)(1)2	Spain	(0)(1)1
(Stojkovic 2)		(Salinas)	

QUARTERFINALS

Italy	(1)1	Ireland	(0)0
(Schillaci)			
Argentina	(0)(0)3	Yugslvia	(0)(0)2
German FR	(1)1	Czchslvkia	(0)0
England	(1)(2)3	Cameroon	(0)(2)2
(Platt, Lineker 2)		(Kunde, Ekeke Belle)	

SEMIFINALS

Argentina	(0)(1)4	Italy	(1)(1)3
(Caniggia)		(Schillaci)	
Grmn FR	(1)(1)5	England	(0)(1)4
(Brehme)		(Lineker)	

THIRD PLACE GAME

Italy	(0)2	England	(0)1
(Baggio, Schillaci)		(Platt)	

FINAL (Rome, 7/8/90)

German FR	(0)1	Argentina	(0)0
(Brehme)			

German FR: Illgner; Brehme; Kohler; Augenthaler; Buchwald; Berthold (Reuter); Littbarski; Haessler; Matthaeus; Voeller; Klinsmann

Argentina: Goycoechea; Lorenzo; Serrizuela; Sensini; Ruggeri (Monzon); Simon; Basualdo; Burruchaga (Calderon); Maradona; Troglio; Dezotti

Referee: Mendez (Mexico)

© Vandystadt/Allsport

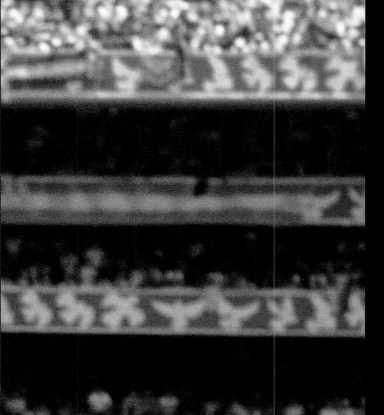

CHAPTER TWO
The Players

S ome of the greatest stars in soccer, men like Alfredo
DiStefano and Hugo Sanchez, never shone as brightly in
World Cup play as was expected of them. Others, like
Gary Lineker and Just Fontaine, seized center stage when
they were supposed to play supporting roles.

   This chapter is about the stars of World Cup play, not necessarily
about the greatest players of all time. And yet, with names like
Pelé, Garrincha, Platini, Puskas, Beckenbauer, and Maradona, it
is about both.

© Syndication International, Ltd.

GORDON BANKS

Gordon Banks leaps "like a salmon out of water" to save a header from Pelé in Mexico, circa 1970.

GORDON BANKS HAD AN UNASSUMING APPEARANCE AND MANNER that belied his abilities. He was 5-foot-11—short by goaltending standards—and not at all fair-haired like England's "Golden Boy," Bobby Moore. His teammates never stopped teasing Banks, affectionately, with the journalistic tag, "World's Greatest Goaltender." Eventually, they came to realize it was Banks who was the most irreplaceable cog in England's World Cup efforts, as he proved with his absence in 1972.

Born in 1939 outside Sheffield, Banks made his fame for the Leicester and Stoke City clubs. He made his debut for England's national team against Brazil in May 1963, when he allowed a curving free kick by Pepé to elude him. Coach Alf Ramsey eventually forgave this great trespass, and Banks was a standout in goal during England's World Cup triumph in 1966.

World-class goalkeepers tend to peak in their thirties, and by the 1970 World Cup in Mexico, Banks was at the top of his game. In a first-round match against Brazil, he made what Pelé called the greatest save he had ever seen. Jairzinho of Brazil centered the ball perfectly, across the goal, to Pelé. Pelé drove the ball down with his head, bouncing it toward the inside of the left post. Since Banks was stationed yards in front of the right post, Pelé immediately began screaming, "Goal!" at his wonderful creation. But Banks dove backwards, upwards, and to the side, all at the same time, knocking the ball over the bar.

"He got up like a salmon out of fresh water," Pelé said, describing Banks' uncanny reaction.

Later in the tournament, before a quarterfinal match against West Germany, Banks drank a tainted beer and suffered from severe gastroenteritis. He was still hobbling the day of the game, leaning hard on the arm of England's physician Neil Phillips. Peter Bonetti replaced him and erred on two balls that led to goals in Germany's 3–2 victory.

Banks continued to play at home, continued to improve, and was named English Footballer of the Year in 1972. He was not only an acrobat in goal, he was a superb, aggressive organizer of the defense in front of him. His international career might have extended well beyond his seventy-three international appearances if he hadn't lost sight in one eye after a car accident.

Eventually, like others of his era, he tried his hand—and his one good eye—at the North American Soccer League, where Banks did his diving and punting for the Fort Lauderdale Strikers.

FRANZ BECKENBAUER

FRANZ BECKENBAUER'S ONLY FLAW AS WEST GERMAN NATIONAL coach was that he expected the sort of style and professionalism from his side that Beckenbauer, the elegant player, once exuded.

"For my generation, playing for one's country was an honor and a wonderful thing," Beckenbauer said. "I see absolutely no reason why that should change. I lay great store on punctuality, exactness and discipline, on things that—like in society—should work smoothly and are able to be taken for granted."

Nobody ever took Beckenbauer's class act for granted. A school-boy star in Munich, Beckenbauer made his Bundesliga debut with

HIS COOL, CONTROLLED GAME AT MIDFIELD OOZED WITH INTELLIGENCE; IT PICKED UP HIS TEAMMATES AT THE MOST CRITICAL MOMENTS.

Bayern Munich at outside left. By age nineteen, in the 1966 World Cup, he was ensconced at midfield. He was asked to mark Bobby Charlton in the final, which robbed Germany of Beckenbauer's offensive creativity and perhaps of the championship.

His cool, controlled game at midfield oozed with intelligence; it picked up his teammates at the most critical moments. In Mexico in 1970, Beckenbauer injured his arm during the final against Italy, then returned to the field and played with his arm in a sling, strapped to his chest. Under his quarterbacking skills, Bayern Munich won three straight European Champions Cups, and Germany won the 1974 World Cup.

Beckenbauer, "The Kaiser," was now an icon in Germany, the inventor of the sweeper position, yet, at age thirty-three, he chose to undergo a very different challenge. He joined the New York Cosmos of the North American Soccer League in 1977, where he became the club's best player and most astute diplomat. While other imported stars maintained a patronizing attitude toward the American player and fan, Beckenbauer was always ready to share his knowledge and insight in unintimidating fashion. It is no wonder the U.S. Soccer Federation, and the 1994 World Cup Organizing Committee, coveted his services during Beckenbauer's incredibly successful reign as West Germany's coach.

His overachieving and undertalented players somehow reached the finals in 1986. Then, given a more mature and creative side in 1990, Beckenbauer won the championship, becoming the first man ever to captain a World Cup titlist on the field, then coach another one from the sidelines. Beckenbauer retired after Italy, looking for new challenges, his eyes on the United States in 1994.

BOBBY CHARLTON

A picture of high-flying football grace, Bobby Charlton attacks against France in a 1966 World Cup match.

BOBBY CHARLTON'S LIFE, HIS FRIENDS SAY, WAS SHAPED BY THE tragedy of February 6, 1958. On that day, the flight carrying Charlton and his talented Manchester United teammates back from a European Cup match against Red Star in Belgrade crashed near Munich. Eight players, eight journalists, a coach, and a trainer were killed. Charlton survived, but the already shy young man retreated further into himself. He would always be the quiet, left-footed wing on England's side, expressing himself fully only on a soccer pitch.

Charlton, the son of a Northumberland miner, was a natural soccer player from birth. It was a hereditary foregone conclusion that he would play soccer, alongside his older brother, Jackie. Bobby Charlton was an exceptional athlete: fast, light-footed, and elegant, with power, range, and a seeing-eye crossing pass. His game developed as he matured, as he was able to play with both feet and to control the pace from midfield on. Charlton made a record 106 international appearances for England, scoring forty-nine goals. He made 606 appearances for Manchester United, his first love, scoring 199 goals.

In 1966, when host England won the World Cup final, Charlton made certain his team would get that far by scoring the only two goals in a 2–1 semifinal win over Portugal. He was named both British Footballer of the Year and European Footballer of the Year in 1966.

Charlton's greatest moment of personal triumph probably came two years later, when Manchester United returned to its pre-crash heights by winning the European Cup. It was a tear-filled experience Charlton shared with his long-time manager, Matt Busby.

Charlton retired from World Cup play after 1970, and from league play in 1973. As a director of Manchester United, he organized a soccer school for local youths, and showed up occasionally doing commentary on the BBC. In 1988, he made a rare appearance in a "Legends Game" at Giants Stadium, near New York City. "I lost half a stone just for this game," he announced, in great spirits and fine physical shape. "I don't get too many chances to play. After you hit fifty, they stop inviting you to these things."

JOHANN CRUYFF

JOHANN CRUYFF'S PHYSICAL APPEARANCE WAS AS DECEPTIVE AND eccentric as his moves on the soccer field. Thin and frail— nicknamed "El Flaco" (Slim) in Spain—Cruyff appeared vulnerable to the slightest whisper of a breeze, let alone a stiff tackle from an Englishman.

Yet Cruyff at his best was virtually untouchable. He was a dangerous striker, yes, but beyond that he was a choreographer. Attacking from midfield, he would lure defenders toward him, then make the deadly pass to his Dutch teammates. He embodied total soccer. He was the hub around which the great Netherlands World Cup team of 1974 spun—all the way to the final.

Cruyff joined the powerful Ajax club when he was only ten and was a starter by age seventeen, in 1964. One year later, he made his

ATTACKING FROM MIDFIELD, HE WOULD LURE DEFENDERS TOWARD HIM, THEN MAKE THE DEADLY PASS TO HIS DUTCH TEAMMATES. HE EMBODIED TOTAL SOCCER.

international debut against Hungary, scoring a goal from midfield. A hot temper belied his angelic looks. In only his second international match against Czechoslovakia, Cruyff struck East German ref Rudi Glockner while gesturing over a dispute. He was suspended for six months.

Cruyff led the Dutch league in scoring in 1967 and 1972, and was named European Footballer of the Year three times—in 1971, 1973, and 1974. In 1973, Cruyff moved to Barcelona, which paid a $1.53 million transfer fee to get him. Cruyff was always very conscious of money—obsessed with it, some would say. His father-in-law was his business manager. Club officials doubled as his tax advisors.

The great orchestrator had other idiosyncrasies. Cruyff was superstitious, always insisting on wearing his uncommon number fourteen uniform. He was stubborn as well, and would not budge when his country beckoned him, desperately, to join the national team for the 1978 World Cup. Eventually, Cruyff, a master of four different languages, left Barcelona to rejoin friend and former coach Rinus Michels with the Los Angeles Aztecs. He scored twenty-five goals in the North American Soccer League, then returned for a brief comeback in Eeyenoord. He is coaching now with his original team, Ajax, having gone full circle in his illustrious, colorful career.

Johann Cruyff in the match that got away: Holland–West Germany, for the 1974 title. Cruyff was the part that made total soccer possible for the Dutch.

© Bettmann/Hulton

Didi, a one-way player with peripheral vision, battles for the ball in a losing cause during the 1954 quarterfinal match against Hungary.

DIDI

VALDIR PEREIRA, OR DIDI, WAS PERHAPS THE ARCHITECT OF MODERN Brazilian soccer. Certainly he came to represent what the national team was all about: midfield flair, pinpoint passing with both feet, and no noticeable desire to tackle or hustle back on defense.

Didi was a dead-ball artist and specialized in the curving free kick, which came to be known as *folha seca* (dry leaf), and later, the banana kick. In 1946, at age eighteen, he began his career with Americano of Campos. He moved to Madureira of Rio, then Fluminense, where he became an effective deep-lying inside-forward. By 1956, two years after his World Cup debut in Switzerland, he was unofficially being called "The World's Greatest Player." This would be a short-lived honor, since Pelé was about to come of age in the same country. But Didi was still the mainstay of the national team, and led Brazil through the World Cup qualifiers for Sweden in 1958.

By 1956, two years after his World Cup debut in Switzerland, he was unofficially being called, "The World's Greatest Player."

There was some talk about leaving Didi off the 1958 national team, because by age thirty his temperament and lifestyle had ruffled a few stuffy Brazilian federation officials. Among his offenses, Didi had married a white woman. "It would be funny if they left me out," Didi said. "After I had paid for their ticket."

He needn't have worried. National coach Vincente Feola included Didi, and Didi repaid him with a string of uncanny playmaking moves. He scored the go-ahead goal in a 5–2 semifinal victory over France. His lead passes over the backs of defenders to Pelé, Vava, and Garrincha laid the groundwork for Brazil's first World Cup title.

After Sweden, Didi played briefly with Real Madrid, where he warred with moody Argentine expatriate Alfredo di Stefano. He eventually returned to Botafogo in 1960, winning two league titles and regaining a spot on the national team at age thirty-four for the 1962 World Cup in Chile. Again, Didi choreographed a World Cup title for Pelé and company, the second in four years.

Unlike other world-class players who have been remarkable failures later as coaches, Didi proved to be an inventive teacher. After coaching Sporting Cristal in Lima, he brought a rejuvenated Peruvian team to Mexico in 1970—giving Brazil all it could handle in the quarterfinals. He then moved on to more exotic places, like Argentina, Turkey, and even Saudi Arabia. Wherever he coaches, Didi imparts some of his creative flair on the players. There has never been a cautious bone in his resilient body.

Eusebio

FOR A BRIEF, SHINING MONTH IN ENGLAND IN 1966, IT SEEMED AS IF Eusebio of Portugal, already nicknamed the "Black Panther," was ready to wrest the "King of Soccer" title from Pelé. There were already remarkable similarities among the two men—in both their flamboyant skills and humble beginnings.

Eusebio, one year younger than Pelé, grew up in Loureco Marques, Mozambique, so poor that he was unable to buy himself a pair of shoes. He played soccer barefoot until he found a single soccer boot that he would put first on one foot, then the other. He signed his first pro contract in 1956 at age fifteen, and was just thrilled to get a new pair of boots for a bonus. Eventually, scouts from Benfica, the top team in Portugal, brought him from Africa to Europe.

Then came 1966. Pelé was injured in a first-round World Cup match. Eusebio filled the superstar breach, scoring nine goals during the tournament and leading Portugal to a third-place finish. In a quarterfinal match against North Korea, Eusebio scored four goals to erase a 3–0 deficit. His fluid presence, his powerful right foot, and his instant acceleration were breathtaking. If he was not quite the instinctive playmaker that Pelé was, he seemed to be more dangerous—if that was possible—around the goalmouth.

The World Cup ended, however, and Eusebio turned into a pumpkin at age twenty-five. There was a humbling 4–0 loss by Benfica to Pelé's Santos team in New York, in which Pelé totally dominated his would-be successor. A succession of knee operations

Eusebio, The Black Panther, is shadowed by Hungarian defenders in a 1966 match. Before injuries and weight problems slowed him, Eusebio was an awesome presence on the pitch.

and injuries sapped Eusebio's skills and his willpower. He earned the reputation, perhaps deserved, of not always giving 100 percent to the cause.

By 1975, Eusebio's value had so diminished that he signed a part-time pact with the Boston Minutemen of the North American Soccer League for a measly $25,000—$4.674 million less than Pelé's contract. Eusebio later hooked on with the second-tier American Soccer League before finally returning to Portugal in an official capacity. In the long run, Eusebio could not compete with Pelé—and never wanted to.

"I feel that calling me the new Pelé is very unfair," Eusebio had said after the 1966 World Cup. "To me, Pelé is the greatest player of all time. I only hope that one day I can be the second-best ever."

During one month in England, he was at least that.

JUST FONTAINE

HIS RECORD OF THIRTEEN GOALS STANDS TODAY, A MARK THAT MIGHT NEVER BE BROKEN.

OTHERS HAVE BEEN FLASHIER, FASTER, MORE POWERFUL, AND MORE durable. But none has scored thirteen goals in a single World Cup tournament, as French striker Just Fontaine managed in 1958.

Born in Marrakesh, Morocco, in 1933, Fontaine played briefly with Casablanca before debuting with Nice, France. By 1956 he had transferred to Rheims, where he gained tremendous personal and international success over the next three seasons. But it was only when another inside-forward, Rene Bliard, was injured that a spot on France's 1958 World Cup team was assured for Fontaine. He would take his place alongside Raymond Kopa and Roger Piantoni on the attack—France's latest version of the Three Musketeers.

A superb poacher with a driving shot, Fontaine scored three goals in his World Cup debut against Paraguay. He scored two in a quarterfinal match against Ireland, two against Yugoslavia, one against Scotland, another against Brazil in a losing semifinal, and four against West Germany in a third-place match at Gothenburg. His record of thirteen goals stands today, a mark that might never be broken.

Fontaine continued his run of success after the World Cup, capitalizing on every defensive error in international play. In a series of exhibitions, he scored hat tricks against Austria and Spain, and two more goals against Chile. Then, in 1959, he suffered a double fracture in his left leg. He came back briefly in 1960, but again suffered a broken leg and retired at the still-tender age of twenty-eight. In just twenty-one international matches, Fontaine had tallied a remarkable thirty goals.

After his premature departure from the game, Fontaine went into sportswriting, then coached the French National team for two matches, and went on to manage a Toulouse youth team.

GARRINCHA

THE LIFE OF MANUEL FRANCISCO DOS SANTOS WAS PAINTED IN mythical colors from birth. Growing up in the Brazilian mountain village of Pau Grande, outside Rio de Janeiro, Manuel would shoot at the little birds, called "Garrincha," that fluttered overhead. He suffered from polio as a child, and one leg was distorted. An operation was required just to enable him to walk.

From these sad, provincial roots grew the greatest dribbler of any era. By age fourteen, he had joined the local club in Pau Grande as an inside-left. In 1953, at age nineteen, he tried out and made the Botafogo club in Rio. Since there was only an opening for a wing, Garrincha accepted the challenge—and never really changed positions again.

Garrincha's international record was astonishing. In fifty-one appearances for Brazil, he lost only one match. He was not originally on the 1958 World Cup team, but teammates Didi and Nilto demanded his selection and he set up two goals in the triumphant final against Sweden.

In 1962, with Pelé injured and the other great Brazilians aging, Garrincha was the whole show—a national hero. He scored two goals against England and Bobby Moore's vaunted defense. He scored two more against Chile in the semifinals. His play was pivotal in the final victory over Czechoslovakia. Garrincha simply possessed too many weapons for defenders. Despite his uneven gait, he was incredibly fast and deceptive on the flank. He could head the ball, curl a shot, or accurately hit the long, low cross.

IN 1962, WITH PELÉ INJURED AND THE OTHER GREAT BRAZILIANS AGING, GARRINCHA WAS THE WHOLE SHOW— A NATIONAL HERO.

After his great triumph in Chile, Garrincha was injured. Doctors discovered that his knee joints were deteriorating, and advised him to rest. But his club team, Botafogo, was going on tour and required his services in order to claim the money promised to them for appearing; this money hinged on their showing up with their star player. Garrincha went, and was never the same. He transferred to Corinthians Paulista in 1966, and then to Flamengo, Bungu, and Portuguesa Santista. He kept playing because he had been a fool with his money and had very little left.

In the midst of his journeyman adventures, Garrincha ran off with a nightclub singer, leaving his wife and eight children behind. Needless to say, this did not help his endorsement status at home or abroad. The singer divorced him, costing him a great deal of money and misery. Garrincha played on, now well past his prime, in France, Mexico, and Italy. In 1972, nearly forty years old, he reappeared in Brazil with another team, then finally gave up a few months later. The little bird was, at last, grounded.

Paul Gascoigne

A STAR WAS BORN IN ITALY, ALTHOUGH HE MIGHT NOT EXPLODE until USA '94. England's young Paul Gascoigne, who turned twenty-three just days before the start of Italia '90, captured the imagination of all who watched his hard, direct play. Soccer fans, watch for this young man in future years.

Gascoigne, a midfielder for Tottenham, was not expected to be an impact player for Coach Bobby Robson in 1990. But when captain Bryan Robson went out with an injury, Gascoigne stepped into the breach in a big way. His forays down the left wing and his looping, accurate lead passes made England very dangerous indeed.

"He was the best young player in the tournament, as far as I'm concerned," said Bobby Robson. "I'm just sorry we couldn't have him for our finale."

Gascoigne was unable to play in England's consolation loss to Italy because he had accumulated a second yellow card in the semi-final draw (a shootout defeat) to West Germany. Gascoigne was some sight to behold in that match, challenging every ball, pushing the tempo up to an almost unbearable level.

© David Cannon/Allsport

There is one thing more about Gascoigne. He feeds off the pressure of the moment, off the fans. With his punk hairdo and rock-hard body, a few journalists noted that he might be mistaken for one of England's hooligan supporters with the addition of a well-placed tattoo or two. At the World Cup, Gascoigne often found time to pump his fists or urge on England's fans in the stands, saluting them when each match was done.

Gascoigne, not one to be beaten or knocked off any ball, will be interacting with his fans for years to come. He is for real, a symbol of England's soccer glory, past and future.

Paul Gascoigne dashes past a Cameroon defender during the 1990 quarterfinal—perhaps the best match of the tournament.

SERGIO GOYCOECHEA

Sergio Goycoechea celebrates after saving a penalty kick against Yugoslavia. These shootout heroics turned a reserve player into a national icon.

ARGENTINIAN GOALTENDER SERGIO GOYCOECHEA WAS ALARMINGLY late to react on crosses. Sometimes, he slapped at balls he should have caught and punted when he should have thrown.

A month before the 1990 World Cup, before Nery Pumpido broke his leg in the second match in Italy, Goycoechea was not Argentina's starting goalie. A year earlier, Goycoechea was not good enough to play for his club team, River Plate, and was exiled to Milonairios of Colombia.

None of this would matter in Italy, because Goycoechea would stop penalty kicks, and that was what the 1990 World Cup was all about. The twenty-seven-year-old scrub goalie was remade, one of those instant stars invented by the twists and turns of an event.

In successive shootout finishes against Yugoslavia and Italy, Goycoechea stopped four of the ten penalties taken against him. A fifth shot by Yugoslavia banged off the woodwork, so he allowed only five goals in ten penalty shots, as Argentina marched on to the final against West Germany. The expected success rate in these gladiatorial showdowns from twelve yards is about 80 percent in favor of the kicker.

"It is not my specialty, but penalty kicks are not at all luck," Goycoechea said. "Some goalkeepers are good at stopping them.

"I think very little," Goycoechea said of his strategy when facing the penalty taker. "The goalkeeper is more calm in this situation. The responsibility is on the player kicking the ball.

"If the goalie jumps the right way, people say what a good stop it was. If he jumps the other way, people say what a good penalty kick it was and the shooter should make them. You have nothing to lose."

For his four headlong diving achievements, Goycoechea became that rarest of novelties: a South American goalie in the spotlight. In all the years of glory for Brazil, Argentina, and Uruguay, there was never much focus on the man minding the net. Who wanted to watch Felix, when there was Pelé?

Goycoechea was not certain that Argentinian coach Carlos Bilardo would select him as a substitute behind Pumpido for the national team. He had his suspicions, however. "I didn't think he had too many alternatives," Goycoechea said. "We don't really have too many great goaltenders in Argentina."

But at Italia '90, Goycoechea became the man who stops penalty kicks.

MARIO KEMPES

THE SIX-GOAL STAR OF THE 1978 WORLD CUP IN ARGENTINA, MARIO Kempes was the left-footed attacker who passed his nation's scoring baton to Diego Maradona.

Kempes made his debut in World Cup competition in 1974 at the tender age of nineteen, when he was not quite ready for the spotlight. Playing center-forward, he blew a breakaway opportunity against Poland during a 3–2 defeat that demoralized Argentina and softened it for the second round.

But by 1978, Kempes was a well-honed, mature scoring machine for Valencia of Spain. Since he was unable to return to Argentina

KEMPES HAD DISPLAYED ENORMOUS COMPOSURE AND HEADINESS UNDER THE GREATEST PRESSURE IMAGINABLE: OVERTIME OF A WORLD CUP FINAL.

for every game, the national team floundered during international exhibitions and his countrymen worried that he might not fit in with the program. There was great debate before the tournament as to whether Kempes should play forward or behind the front row of three strikers, as he had with Valencia. In the end, he did a little of both, handling both positions brilliantly.

After a slow start, Kempes awoke in the second round. He scored the only two goals in a match against Poland—one on a brilliant header from a Daniel Bertoni cross. He scored two more against Peru in a shocking 6–0 rout that allowed Argentina to edge past Brazil on goal differential and into the finals.

In the final against Holland, Kempes assured himself of immortality with two headlong dashes that produced two of Argentina's three goals. Marked loosely by Willy Van de Kerkhof (many observers felt Johan Neeskens should have been assigned the task), Kempes scored the first goal in the thirty-eighth minute with a booming left-footer. In overtime, he dribbled through the penalty area and beat goalie Jan Jongbloed. Kempes had displayed enormous composure and headiness under the greatest pressure imaginable: overtime of a World Cup final.

By 1982, now a bit past his prime, Kempes was out on the left flank and no longer the focus of the Argentinian attack. That was now Maradona's burden to carry.

Even in his waning years, Mario Kempes was still able to attack; here he is attacking Italy in the 1982 World Cup finals.

© Bob Thomas Sports Photography

Golden Head had platinum feet, as well. Sandor Kocsis performs a scissors kick, and earns a perfect ten in style points.

SANDOR KOCSIS

ONE OF THE MAGIC MAGYARS IN THE FIFTIES, SANDOR KOCSIS WAS the artistic counterpoint to Ferenc Puskas' driving, overpowering game. Kocsis scored eleven goals playing inside-right for Hungary during the 1954 World Cup, and finished his international career with seventy-five goals and seven hat tricks—a world record he shares only with Pelé.

Kocsis was smaller and more frail than his teammate Puskas, but he was so acrobatic and effective in the air that he was nicknamed "Golden Head"—this despite the fact that Kocsis' thick hair was decidedly black.

Kocsis joined the Hungarian club Ferencvaros at the age of nineteen in 1948, and quickly led that team to the league title. He transferred to the army team, Honved, in 1950, where he was teamed with such greats as Puskas and halfback Joszef Bozsik. In the first round of the 1954 World Cup in Switzerland, Kocsis scored four goals against West Germany. He scored another against Brazil in the quarterfinals and two critical goals in the semifinal against Uruguay. After the tournament, he was given a special cup created in Mexico for the leading scorer in the tournament. Kocsis graciously accepted the honor, but came under fire from hard-line Hungarian authorities who condemned "the cult of the individual."

HE WAS SO ACROBATIC AND EFFECTIVE IN THE AIR THAT HE WAS NICKNAMED "GOLDEN HEAD"—THIS DESPITE THE FACT THAT KOCSIS' THICK HAIR WAS DECIDEDLY BLACK.

After the revolution in 1956, he defected with most of the Honved team touring in South America. He showed up next as a player-coach for Young Fellows in Switzerland, then signed with Barcelona for the 1957–58 season. Stodgy FIFA, however, banned him at first because of his status as a fugitive from Honved. Eventually, in 1958, he began a string of successful seasons that ended in 1966, when he retired gracefully and was given a noteworthy testimonial.

Kocsis worked as a coach for a few minor Spanish clubs, putting his graceful skills on display every so often for Barcelona's veteran team.

GRZEGORZ LATO

AT THE 1974 WORLD CUP IN WEST GERMANY, RIGHT-WING GRZEGORZ Lato and his Polish teammates burst surprisingly onto the soccer scene as the only aesthetic equals of the Dutch. It was Lato's duty, simply put, to lurk and poach in the penalty area, where he was usually spotted by left-wing Robert Gadocha in time to pull off a pass from the wing into the center of the field, usually in front of the goal, otherwise known as a cross. Although Lato played for Stal Mielec and Gadocha for Legia, the two players looked as if they had played uncountable matches as teammates.

Grzegorz Lato heads—where else?—for the goal. No doubt, Robert Gadocha, Lato's private servicer, is nearby.

After scoring four goals in the first round—including two during a stunning 3–2 win over Argentina—Lato continued his surge into the semifinal round. He scored the only goal of the game against Sweden on a header from—who else?—Gadocha. Against Yugoslavia, he netted the winning goal in a 2–1 victory on another header. His streak was stopped momentarily in what amounted to a losing semifinal match against West Germany, but only after a lovely save by goalie Sepp Maier. Lato scored his seventh goal, more than any other player in the 1974 tournament, against Brazil in the third-place match.

Lato played in two more World Cups for Poland, with decreasing effectiveness. He scored the only goal against Tunisia in a first-round match, and another against Brazil in a second-rounder in 1978. But Lato was already displaced as chief goalmaker by Zbigniew Boniek. By 1982, Lato was playing midfield for a Belgian club when he was recalled by the Polish team for the World Cup in Spain. He was asked to be a table-setter now, and he was most effective jogging at midfield, reading the seams in opponents' defenses. When Boniek was suspended for the semifinal match against Italy, Lato was moved up to the striker position one last time. But he was slowed by age and injury, and without Gadocha around, he was not about to get the ball in his favorite positions.

LEONIDAS

WHEN LEONIDAS DA SILVA ARRIVED IN FRANCE FOR THE 1938 WORLD Cup, South American soccer was still something of an enigma to European fans. By the time he left, eight goals later, it was a total mystery. How could a man, or any vertebrate, curl around a soccer ball like this?

The diminutive Brazilian center-forward, nicknamed "O Homen Borracha" (The Rubber Man), startled everybody in 1938 with his contortionist abilities. Leonidas invented the bicycle kick, which he could pull off with either foot. He was capable of such ball-control tricks, and such acceleration, that few defenders dared to challenge him directly. They merely attempted to cut down his options.

Leonidas was born in 1913, and fulfilled his early promise at age eighteen, when he scored two goals for Brazil in his international

THE DIMINUTIVE BRAZILIAN CENTER-FORWARD, NICKNAMED "O HOMEN BORRACHA" (THE RUBBER MAN), STARTLED EVERYBODY IN 1938 WITH HIS CONTORTIONIST ABILITIES.

debut against Uruguay. The Uruguayans were appropriately impressed. He signed with Nacional Montevideo, and won the Uruguyan national title in 1933. He returned to Brazil, to club teams Vasco da Gama, then Botafogo, then Flamengo, then São Paulo. During this span, his eight goals led Brazil to a third-place finish in the 1938 World Cup and he became a national hero of unprecedented renown.

Leonidas was the subject of songs, dances, films, and poems. His stature would have grown even greater, perhaps approaching Pelé's eventual pedestal, if World War II had not deprived him of a world showcase for his skills. From age twenty-five to thirty-seven, which included at least six peak seasons, Leonidas had no World Cup to attend. He finally retired from soccer in 1950, became the manager of São Paulo, and then later a radio commentator. Eventually, after Brazil had produced other soccer heroes to take his place, Leonidas slipped out of the limelight entirely and operated a furniture store in São Paulo.

GARY LINEKER

IN TWO WORLD CUPS MARKED BY LOW SCORING AND DISAPPOINTING strikers, forward Gary Lineker of England scored a total of ten goals and carried his team to the semifinals of the 1990 tournament in Italy. Lineker, a relative unknown before 1986, thus became a top-ranked international superstar.

This whirlwind transition occurred at the 1986 World Cup in Mexico, where Lineker led all scorers with six goals and proved himself a world-class striker. Born and raised in Leicester, he left that town's club team for Everton over a contract dispute. His goal-scoring ability had already helped lift Leicester to the first division, and he tallied thirty goals for Everton during the 1985–86 season. There were still some critics, however, who argued that his statistics were not true indicators of any real accomplishment. Even his six goals in nine international appearances were suspect, since three had come against Turkey and two against the United States—clearly inferior sides.

Lineker's selection to the English World Cup team in 1986 was by no means assured. When he was finally chosen, it was understood

by all that Lineker would have to prove himself in order to retain his spot. He did so emphatically, with a hat trick against Poland and three other goals. All debate about his worth ceased. Following the World Cup, he was immediately signed by Barcelona, which paid a fanciful $4.2 million in transfer fees to Everton for his bread-and-butter services. Eventually, Lineker ended up back with an English club at Tottenham.

In Italy, now a mainstay on England's side with thirty-one goals and fifty international appearances, Lineker scored four times, third best in the tournament. He scooted down the middle of the box with his own chest trap, and beat Ireland goalie Patrick Bonner in the opening match. He scored two penalty kicks in England's 3–2 comeback win over Cameroon in the quarterfinals, and he nailed a left-foot shot against West Germany late in a losing semifinal.

Lineker is not a showman, not in the sense of Pelé. He is not a playmaker, not like Platini. He has more medals for snooker competitions than he does from his soccer career. Yet his nice touch around the goal mouth, his speed, his nose for the ball, and his accuracy were good enough to make him a star for two summer months in 1986 and 1990, when the whole world was watching.

LINEKER LED ALL SCORERS WITH SIX GOALS AND PROVED HIMSELF A WORLD-CLASS STRIKER.

DIEGO MARADONA

IN 1986, DIEGO MARADONA WAS THE HERO, THE ARTIST, THE UNSTOPPABLE goal scorer. In 1990, he was the villain, the cheat, the superstar without a single score.

So go the extremes of soccer, and of the petulant Maradona. From the time when, as a young boy, he bounced a soccer ball skyward to bewitch an audience, Maradona demanded the spotlight. He was afforded one, as long as his incredible ballhandling skills held out.

At his best, marked loosely in the open field, Maradona was a genius, a fireplug with a low center of gravity and a balletic bullishness. Nobody could tackle him fairly. He could dribble past any defender, score off any goaltender. He had five goals in 1986, when he led Argentina past West Germany in the World Cup final.

But already, controversy dogged him. There was the "hand of God" goal against England, a quick tap of the ball with Maradona's

open hand unseen by the referee. England screamed, but talkative Maradona called this divine intervention.

In the four years between his two Cup appearances, Maradona did nothing to keep a low profile. He signed a multi-million dollar contract with Napoli in Italy, then took extended vacations and grew overweight. He staged a wildly elaborate wedding, and showed little dedication toward anything but personal excess.

Still, he could play the sport. He led Napoli to two league titles, becoming a favorite of the outcast Neapolitans. Nobody could be sure what to expect from Maradona, or Argentina, at Italia '90. What they eventually saw was outrageous, effective, and very nearly successful.

In the second match, Maradona got away with another handball, this time against the Soviets in his own penalty box, causing coach Valery Lobanovsky to scream, "If a referee misses this penalty, he should not be a referee." Maradona dribbled past three defenders, setting up a goal by Claudio Caniggia against Brazil, and a major 1–0 upset in the second round. Maradona played in Naples against Italy in the semifinal, announcing that the rest of Italy "will never share a victory with the Neapolitans. For 364 days, they are not part of Italy. It is a slap in the face."

Finally, overwhelmed by superior competition, exaggerating fouls against himself to earn yellow cards for opponents, Mara-

Above: *By 1990, Diego Maradona was more theatrics than heroics. But he was still enough of a threat to worry even mighty Germany in the final.* Below: *Just six? These Belgian defenders were no problem for Maradona, back in 1982.*

dona's Argentina fell to West Germany in the final. But again, not without controversy.

Before the match, Maradona got into a scuffle with Italian police who were questioning his brother about ownership of a Ferrari. Maradona charged "conspiracy" and later blamed the Mafia for a penalty-kick call against Argentina in the final. Clearly, Maradona was no Pelé, no Beckenbauer, no diplomat.

"I am not trying to be Pelé," Maradona said. "I will settle for being the best player in Argentina."

That much is assured.

LOTHAR MATTHAEUS

LOTHAR MATTHAEUS OF WEST GERMANY WAS THE MIDFIELD CHESS-master of the 1990 World Cup, a twenty-nine-year-old strategist who penetrated defenses in Italy or devised the plans to do so.

Matthaeus was not as flashy as attacking teammates Juergen Klinsmann or Rudi Voeller, but he was certainly as valuable; proba-

Lothar Matthaeus launches another assault, thinking and dribbling on the run.

© Billy Stickland/Allsport

bly more so. Matthaeus distributed the ball, decided when the back pass was in order, when it was time to streak, directly, toward the goal. His coolness under pressure was apparent from the start, and it was Matthaeus, the captain, who was asked to speak for the team in victory.

"This is the end of a dream," said Matthaeus, who immediately headed for an extended vacation on the island of Mauritius off Africa. "The perfect ending."

While dreaming and scheming in Italy, Matthaeus found time to score four times, including two goals against Yugoslavia and the only goal in a quarterfinal match against Czechoslovakia.

"That is not his job, but he has shown what a superstar he has become in all facets," said West German coach Franz Beckenbauer. "He has superseded Diego Maradona as the star of the 1990 World Cup."

Beckenbauer conveniently forgot Italian attacker Salvatore Schillaci, but his point was well taken. Matthaeus, veteran of three World Cups and sixteen World Cup matches, had a wonderful Cup, a tournament in which he set the attacking tempo with his accurate passing and rushes to open space. Matthaeus knew teammates Klinsmann and Voeller well, since all three are teammates on InterMilan. When it came time to service them, Matthaeus did so on a silver platter that led to the golden trophy.

STANLEY MATTHEWS

SIR STANLEY MATTHEWS OF ENGLAND WAS UNMATCHED IN TWO VITAL areas: ball control and durability. This first quality was not unconnected with the second, since his deft touch allowed him to stay in the sport and remain effective until the ridiculous age of fifty-two.

Matthews began his career at age seventeen for Stoke City, then made Blackpool famous. He was playing for England's national side by age nineteen, in 1934, but the English Football Association elected not to participate in the World Cup until after the war, in 1950. By this time, Matthews was thirty-five years old and still the best right-wing in the game.

He was also an elder statesman, of sorts, among the English players, and did not appreciate the meddling from new coach Walter

HIS DEFT TOUCH ALLOWED HIM TO STAY IN THE SPORT AND REMAIN EFFECTIVE UNTIL THE RIDICULOUS AGE OF FIFTY-TWO.

Stanley Matthews, finished with his dash down the wing,
readies his deadly crossing pass.

Winterbottom. "He's not letting players go out and play their own game," Matthews said. Winterbottom did not agree. In fact, he did his best to keep Matthews off the team. But in the final weeks before the 1950 World Cup in Brazil, Matthews was recalled by popular demand. This was to be the pattern of the tournament. Winterbottom would drop Matthews from the starting squad. England would get in trouble. Matthews would be restored for the next game. Finally, Winterbottom went too far, benching Matthews before the most humiliating encounter in England's soccer history: a 1–0 loss to the United States.

Four years passed; Matthews was now thirty-nine, and the same silly World Cup mind game was played between himself and Winterbottom. Matthews was recalled again to Brazil at the last moment, eventually providing England's finest playmaking moments in a 4–2 quarterfinal loss to Uruguay. Thrown by Winterbottom into the inside-left position, Matthews' footwork was so inspiring that the South American crowd chanted, "Matt-hews, Matt-hews" each time he touched the ball.

By 1958, at age forty-three, Matthews was ignored by England's selection committee. His continued domination back home was now a bit of an embarrassment. He continued to play for another nine years, treating the ball on the dribble as if it were an extension of his own foot. For his uncanny skills, displayed for two generations of British soccer fans, Matthews was knighted by the queen.

ROGER MILLA

ROGER MILLA WAS IN SEMIRETIREMENT, PLAYING FOR THE INDIAN Ocean island club of Jeunesse St. Pierroise, when the vision struck him. He would go back to Cameroon, at age thirty-eight, and rejoin the national team in time for the 1990 World Cup in Italy.

This idea of Milla's met some resistance from his old teammates in Cameroon and from members of that nation's sports federation who had helped stage Milla's farewell night some three years earlier. He had, after all, missed all of Cameroon's qualifying matches and shown no evidence of being fit in a world-class fashion. Nonetheless, with the help of Cameroon President Paul Biya and the support of old fans in his native country, Milla was added to the national team as a reserve.

What followed was pure drama and joy, with Milla driving home four goals for Cameroon and sparking his country's drive to the World Cup quarterfinals.

"I could not imagine anything like this," Milla said. "But the people of my country, they saw that this would happen."

Coming off the bench against Romania in a scoreless match at Bari, Milla tallied twice in a matter of eleven minutes, assuring a 2-1 victory and Cameroon's advancement into the second round. Against Colombia in Naples, again off the bench, he came racing, unabashed, through the middle, shook off two defenders, and beat goaltender Rene Higuita. Milla danced the lambada at the corner spot, and he was not finished. Just two minutes later he stole the ball from wandering goalie Higuita, allowed himself a slight smile, then stroked a shot into the open net for his fourth goal.

By now a hero not only in Cameroon but in all of Africa, Milla still had another night of heroics left in his wiry, nimble body. Against England in perhaps the best match of the tournament, Milla again entered the quarterfinal game at the half and set up two quick goals by teammates that temporarily gave Cameroon the 2-1 lead.

Milla's success was an inspiration, and suddenly he was talking about playing again professionally in Spain, or Italy, or anywhere that would have a thirty-eight-year-old player going on twenty-five. "The appetite grows as you eat," Milla said. General managers are not always romantics, and there were no immediate offers from top European sides. Still, Milla will always have Naples.

Roger Milla, age thirty-eight and definitely un-retired, on his way to one of two goals against Colombia in a second-round match at Naples in the 1990 World Cup.

© Vandystadt/Allsport

BOBBY MOORE

SUCH WAS THE SACROSANCT STATUS OF THE ENGLISH TEAM'S WORLD Cup captain, Bobby Moore, back in 1970 that his prosecution— or persecution—in Bogota, Colombia, became an election issue at home.

Moore was accused of stealing a $1,300 bracelet from a Bogota jewelry store while England was on a pre-World Cup tour through South America. (''Steal a bracelet?'' said teammate Alan Mullery. "With Bobby's money, he could have bought the shop.") Moore was arrested and held in Bogota for five days while the English Parliament and Prime Minister Harold Wilson screamed long and loud for his release as elections approached. In the House of Commons, Peter Bessell, a liberal, shouted, "It is outrageous that the finest football team in the world should be treated to malicious attacks." Wilson, a conservative, countered by ordering the British embassy in Bogota to take action.

Just as protests reached a fever pitch among the English population, Moore was released. Eventually, charges were dropped. Yet some British fans have never forgiven Colombia, and South America in general, for what it did to their Golden Boy—the glamorous player as famous for his hair cream advertisements as his soccer.

Bobby Moore, England's Golden Boy, faces down a worthy adversary in the 1966 final—Franz Beckenbauer.

© Allsport

more goals for the Fort Lauderdale Strikers of the North American Soccer League. By this time, a long way from Zinsen, Muller's reputation could survive even the ill-fated NASL.

JOHAN NEESKENS

JOHAN NEESKENS PLAYED SOCCER AT AN UNDYING, FRENETIC pace. The Dutch midfielder attacked when his team was on offense; tackled when his team was on defense. He was rarely out of the play, or the picture.

He was a perfect match for superstar Johann Cruyff and Holland's "total soccer" revolution of the seventies. He was a player who wanted the ball and knew what to do with it when he got it. Success followed Neeskens. With Cruyff, he led Ajax of Amsterdam to three consecutive European Cup titles from 1971 to 1973. He was second banana only to Cruyff on the World Cup team in 1974, when the Netherlands was clearly the superior side to winner West Germany. He was the team leader in Holland's second-place finish in 1978.

Neeskens was as adventurous off the field as on, which led him to an international career (he can speak English, Spanish, and Dutch) and at least one ugly confrontation. After five years with Barcelona, he spurned offers from England and France to sign a $1.6 million contract with the New York Cosmos in June 1979. Still near his peak at age twenty-seven, he was thrown together with stern West German coach Hennes Weisweiler. This was war from the start, with the impatient Weisweiler eventually suspending Neeskens for missing a team flight. Their conflict went deeper than that, of course. It had to do with personality and with soccer style. Neeskens, a favorite with the New York fans, eventually won reinstatement after eleven long months.

Neeskens signed a contract with Ajax when he was just sixteen. He probably could have been a striker, because his shot was strong and his nerves steady. In Barcelona, he once converted twenty-two penalty kicks in a row. But Neeskens wanted to be involved in all play, not just the offense.

"I will play anywhere I am told," Neeskens once said while with the Cosmos. "But I want always to play in the middle."

From out of midfield and an opponent's nightmare: Johan Neeskens, pushing the ball upfield.

© Bob Thomas Sports Photography

PELÉ

"WHATEVER FIELD OF ENDEAVOR THIS MAN ENTERED, PHYSICAL OR MENTAL, HE WOULD BE A GENIUS," DECLARED DR. HILTON GOSLING, A BRAZILIAN PSYCHOLOGIST.

Pelé weaving through traffic—and a few helpless Englishmen—in a 1970 World Cup match.

THEY COME, THEY GO. GREAT PLAYERS WITH LIGHTNING SPEED and thunderous shots. But there is still only one Pelé.

"He is the king; the most, the great untouchable," said the fine English defender, Bobby Moore. "Pelé is capable of converting millions to soccer."

His is the story of soccer, of Brazil, of the artist. Edson Arantes do Nascimento was born in the small Brazilian interior town of Tres Coracoes (Three Hearts), the son of a part-time soccer player. He grew up sharing a two-bedroom house with six other family members, kicking around a sock filled with rags—and sometimes a grapefruit—in the streets. By age fourteen he played on his father's team, Bauru. By age fifteen, in 1955, his father had secured a job for him with Santos, under coach Luiz Alonso Perez, for $75 a month. In his first game for Santos, he scored four goals, and received a $1,000 bonus.

"Pelé is not only the greatest player I ever coached," said Perez, "he is the greatest player anyone ever coached."

His feats are legendary. He scored six goals at the 1958 World Cup and twelve goals in his World Cup career, but he was never a one-dimensional striker. He was an attacking choreographer, both a starter and a finisher of plays. In 1966 at England, he scored an impossible curling free kick against Bulgaria. The Bulgarians then took him out of the match, and the tournament, with brutal tackles. The Brazilians immediately lost all focus and their next match to Hungary.

Pelé's ball control and his breathtaking rushes were made possible by a unique meld of mind and physiology. Tests run by the Brazilians on their superman in 1966 showed that his heart beat fifty-six to fifty-eight times per minute and that his peripheral vision was 30 percent better than the average athlete. "Whatever field of endeavor this man entered, physical or mental, he would be a genius," declared Dr. Hilton Gosling, a Brazilian psychologist.

The Brazilians declared Pelé a "national treasure" and deflected offers from other countries for his services. Italian teams offered $2 million to Santos. Santos, and Pelé, wouldn't budge. Finally, on June 11, 1975, when he was well past his World Cup prime, Pelé accepted a $4.7 million offer to play in New York with the Cosmos. There was great teeth-gnashing in Brazil, and some fanatics have yet to forgive him (especially after he suggested in 1988 that he was happy the United States was awarded the 1994 World Cup, even though it was over Brazil). In America, Pelé sparked a mammoth, albeit temporary, surge in interest in the North American Soccer League.

"Today, soccer has arrived in the United States," Pelé declared to the world upon his signing a contract with the Cosmos. "Spread the word."

Today, he remains soccer's greatest diplomat, a man who was invited to Buckingham Palace to meet the Queen, was granted a private audience with the Pope ("Don't be nervous, my son," Pope Paul VI told him. "I am more nervous than you."), stopped the Nigerian-Biafran war for one day, and received the French Legion of Honor. Pelé has done all of this, dribbled through four Mexican defenders to score a goal, and won three World Cups for Brazil. He says he will campaign for the presidency of Brazil in 1994, and nobody should bet against him. He has done everything, it seems—except discover the meaning or origin of his nickname. "Pelé" is his one, enduring mystery.

Head, body, and soul: Pelé embodied the great soccer ideal.

SILVIO PIOLA

ONLY WORLD WAR II COULD STOP ITALIAN CENTER-FORWARD Silvio Piola. It did so by putting his World Cup career on hold for the eight years he was the dominant player in Europe, preventing him from attaining the sort of legendary status accorded later stars like Pelé, Michel Platini, and Diego Maradona.

Piola emerged as a soccer force in 1935, debuting for Italy's national side and demonstrating awesome power. He was tall and solid, yet fast and adept enough to rush past all but the fleetest defenders. His game in the air was also unmatched. Major Frank Buckley, the famed English coach, spotted Piola early and declared, "Piola will shortly be the best center-forward in Europe."

Piola made a prophet out of Buckley and a proud dictator out of doting Benito Mussolini. He utterly dominated play at the 1938 World Cup from start to finish. He assisted and scored against Norway in a 2–1 first-round match. Against the French hosts in the second round, Piola scored two goals in the second half—one on a breakaway, one on a header.

In the semifinal match against Brazil, defender Domingos Da Guia became enraged at Piola's elusiveness. After fourteen minutes of humiliation, Da Guia tripped Piola as he was galloping past him in the penalty box. Italy was awarded a penalty kick, which it converted for a solid two-goal lead. In the final against Hungary, Piola scored twice more. This was his tournament.

Before that, though, there would be one more demonstration of his grit and ferocious will. In May 1939, during a match against England in Milan, Piola fell while on the move toward the goal. He managed to punch the ball past the English goalie, then punch right-back George Male in the eye.

Piola continued to play—with decreasing effectiveness—in 566 career appearances in the Italian League. He retired in 1952 and assisted Hungarian Lajor Czeizler in coaching the Italians at the World Cup in Switzerland. This proved to be something of a disaster. The team, freed from the iron hand of coach Vittoria Pozzo, rebelled and performed with no discipline whatsoever.

Piola was a technical advisor with the Italian federation until 1976, then disappeared and was eventually unearthed by journalists who found him living in a slum on a small pension. In his own way, Piola never stopped paying for the inconvenience of world war.

IN MAY 1939 ... [HE] FELL WHILE ON THE MOVE TOWARD THE GOAL. HE MANAGED TO PUNCH THE BALL PAST THE ENGLISH GOALIE, THEN PUNCH RIGHT-BACK GEORGE MALE IN THE EYE.

MICHEL PLATINI

IN 1988, JUST TWO YEARS AFTER LEADING FRANCE TO THE SEMIFINALS of the World Cup tournament in Mexico, Michel Platini played in a nostalgic Legends Game at Giants Stadium a few miles away from New York City. Platini, now thirty-three and perhaps fifteen pounds (6 kg) too heavy around the midsection, waddled around the artificial surface for most of the match. He managed to set up one goal and score another, as Europe diplomatically tied the rest of the world 2–2.

"It is hard for us Europeans," said Platini, puffing on a cigarette after the match in the locker room. "We play the long game, and that is more exhausting."

This whole scene, simultaneously sad and amusing, was a reminder of Platini's amazing technical and intuitive skills. Here was a midfielder of obviously limited physical prowess, of equally questionable fitness, who was able to dominate World Cup play in both Spain and Mexico in 1982 and 1986, to lead Juventus to the World Cup championship, and to earn the European Player of the

Michel Platini goes up against Hungary. Platini, the plotter, was usually more effective with his feet planted on turf.

© Vandystadt/Allsport

Year award three straight years. It was his genius that did all this; his mind for playmaking, his ability to move toward the gap or toward the ball at just the right moment, his sixth sense that allowed him always to avoid the tackle.

Platini's geometric wizardry might not have been encouraged in some coaches' systems, but Platini was fortunate to come of age with Michel Hidalgo at the reins. Platini's first match was also the first for new coach Hidalgo. Hidalgo encouraged Platini's forays, allowed him to ad-lib attacking plays. Platini, the detached technician, calmly surveyed the possibilities before him. Then, he computed and executed the perfect play. This cool reserve made him a favorite of Hidalgo's for the penalty shot, and Platini converted potentially his most important penalty kick to tie West Germany early during France's semifinal loss in 1982.

At his peak in 1986, when Pelé called him "the best, the most complete player in the world today," Platini almost single-handedly knocked out defending World Cup champion Italy with his dominant play and his fortieth career goal for France. Platini scored once more, in a quarterfinal win over Brazil. Then, finally, West Germany tied him into knots with a shadow, Wolfgang Rolff, and the use of an offside trap. Platini retired from World Cup play, heading straight for the nearest cigarette.

FRANTISEK PLANICKA

HE WAS QUITE LIGHT ON HIS FEET, HIS POSITIONING WAS FAULTLESS, AND HIS REACTIONS WERE UNFATHOMABLE. HE LOVED HIS SPORT LIKE FEW OTHER MEN.

FROM HIS YOUTH, SCOUTS IN CZECHOSLOVAKIA UNDERSTOOD THAT Frantisek Planicka could someday stand in goal for his national team. Signed by the lowly Bubanek Club, he joined Slavia as a teenager and stayed with this Prague team for seven hundred matches until he retired from his legendary career.

Between 1925 and 1938—between the two wars that united Czechoslovakia, then tore it brutally apart—Planicka made seventy-four international appearances and was named captain of the national team. There was only one other goaltender in Europe at this time, Ricardo Zamora of Spain, whose name could be whispered in the same sentence with Planicka. But Zamora did not make as great an impact on the World Cup. Planicka had greater teammates, and perhaps a greater sense of the moment.

His Czech team, in fact, nearly stole the World Cup in 1934. If not for a fluke goal scored by Raimondo Orsi in the last minutes of the final, Planicka would have carried the Jules Rimet trophy back to Prague. But it was not 1934 that Planicka would be remembered for; it would be 1938. Then, in back-to-back second-round matches against the Brazilians, Planicka stood his ground against the flashy Leonidas Da Silva despite a broken right arm. The first match ended in a 1–1 overtime draw. Brazil won the replay, finally, 2–1. Planicka's reputation, however, was assured.

Planicka was not particularly tall or physical. He was quite light on his feet, his positioning was faultless, and his reactions were unfathomable. He loved his sport like few other men, and had the sense to retire at the top of his form. He did play, less conspicuously, on veteran teams in Czechoslovakia until he was into his sixties.

FERENC PUSKAS

FERENC PUSKAS WAS THE GREATEST SCORING MACHINE OF HIS generation, and perhaps any generation. He scored eighty-three goals in eighty-four international matches. Those who saw him play for Hungary, and later in Spain, would grant him all the laurel wreaths deserving of a great soccer hero. And yet, Puskas was cheated out of the biggest prize of all, the World Cup title, by a nasty tackle and an aborted revolution.

Puskas, a major in the Hungarian army, was a fireplug of a man, a squat striker whose chief weapon was a thunderous left foot; he rarely used his head or right foot. They were unnecessary appendages. He parted his plastered-down hair in the middle, as if to lower air resistance. He had quick acceleration, unmatched ball control, and tremendous power.

Puskas and brilliant Hungarian teammates like Sandor Kocsis burst onto the international soccer scene, to be made odds-on favorites at the 1954 World Cup in Switzerland. But in the second match of the tournament, Puskas was brutally tackled by big, blond German stopper center-half Werner Liebrich. His ankle was badly sprained and bruised. Puskas watched the rest of the games from the sidelines until the final, when he played on a sore ankle in the rain. He scored one goal and tallied another that was nullified by a

PUSKAS WAS CHEATED OUT OF THE BIGGEST PRIZE OF ALL, THE WORLD CUP TITLE, BY A NASTY TACKLE AND AN ABORTED REVOLUTION.

questionable offside. Hungary lost, 3–2, and Puskas would never have this chance again.

He defected while on a South American tour with his army team, Honved, during the Hungarian revolution. The press reported him dead, but he had fled to Italy, and later continued his career in Spain. At thirty-six years old, deferring to irascible teammate and superstar Alfredo di Stefano, Puskas played for Real Madrid in the 1962 European Cup final in Amsterdam, won by Benfica. He scored three goals in that final, then handed Eusebio his jersey after the match in a wonderful private moment between superstars. Later that year at Chile, Puskas played for Spain's national team in the World Cup and was unimpressed by soccer's evolution.

"Slow, very slow," he said. "I like the kind of game where one wins 5–4, 5–3, or even loses by the same score. Here, they're no longer playing football, it's war." Puskas tried to impart some of his philosophy as a coach in America, in Greece, in Saudi Arabia, and in Chile. He did not always succeed.

LUIGI RIVA

RIVA'S SUCCESS STORY GREW ALL THE MORE COMPELLING AFTER HE CAME BACK FROM TWO BROKEN LEGS.

IN AN ERA OF ITALY'S DREADFULLY CONSERVATIVE *CATENACCIO* tactics Luigi Riva reminded his countrymen that there was still something wonderful out there called offense. Riva was a scoring machine, one of those fine finishers that comes along once every decade or so for a few fortunate, world-class soccer countries.

Orphaned in his youth, Riva overcame all social and physical obstacles to become the dominant center-forward and left-wing of his time. He was famous for his diagonal charge from the flanks into the penalty area, a move that defenders knew was coming, but could somehow do nothing to stop.

In the early 1970s, when Riva was pulling down a 40-million-lira salary and endorsing every product in Italy, his left foot and Gianni Rivera's playmaking were all there was of Italy's World Cup chances. In the qualifying matches leading up to the 1974 World Cup, for example, Riva scored seven of Italy's ten goals. In the 1970 World Cup, when Italy played its way to the final, Riva scored two goals in the quarterfinal against Mexico and another goal in the semifinal against Germany.

© Syndication International, Ltd

Italy's selectors foolishly passed over Riva for the 1966 team, even though he had already taken his club team, Cagliari, into the first division and to a title. Riva, doggedly loyal, stayed on in Sardinia even after wealthy Juventus offered him $2.3 million in 1973. Riva's success story grew all the more compelling after he came back from two broken legs. His running and leaping skills were somewhat diminished, but his striking instincts around the penalty box were not.

GIANNI RIVERA

GIANNI RIVERA WAS A FRAIL ITALIAN MAGICIAN DURING THE LATE sixties and early seventies; in many ways, he was a forerunner of Johann Cruyff. His dominance was so complete, his responsibilities on the national team so encompassing, that he often shouldered the blame for any of Italy's defeats in the World Cup.

This problem came to a head in 1966 at England, when Italy was knocked out in the first round while scoring only two goals in three games. Worse, it was defeated 1–0 by North Korea. Rivera's choreography simply was not working, and the twenty-two-year-old suffered much criticism at home.

The next World Cup, in 1970, was much more successful for Italy and Rivera—although it did not start out that way. Having moved back from inside-forward to attacking midfielder, Rivera found himself in competition for a spot with arch-rival Sandro Mazzola of Inter Milan. He was dropped from the lineup, then reinstated by Artemio Franchi, president of the Italian Federation, after several tantrums on all sides.

This was most fortunate, because Rivera was at his best again. He scored a goal in the quarterfinals against Mexico and assisted on two goals by Luigi Riva. He knocked in the winning goal against West Germany in the semifinals, in overtime. Coach Ferruccio Valcareggi stubbornly refused to use Rivera as a starter in the final against Brazil, and his second-half appearance alongside Mazzola caused only confusion in a 4–1 defeat.

Long before this roller-coaster ride to the World Cup final, Rivera had assured himself a place in the historic annals of Italian soccer. An accurate passer with incredible ball-control skills, Rivera made his debut with Alessandria, where his father, a railroad worker, had raised him. A.C. Milan paid a $182,000 transfer for Rivera, and his brilliant performance against Benfica at Wembley in the European Cup final in 1963, at age nineteen, had sent a message to the entire continent. Rivera led Milan to the league championship in 1968, and was voted the European Footballer of the Year in 1969.

Rivera tired of the political infighting, and retired from the game in 1978 after 127 goals in 514 league appearances. His contract wars with the owners of A.C. Milan were finally over.

PAOLO ROSSI

Opposite page: *Reformed, reborn Paolo Rossi outraces Paulo Falcao of Brazil during a 1982 match.*

PAOLO ROSSI, ITALY'S SMALL, CLEVER, CENTER-FORWARD, FOUND redemption at the 1982 World Cup.

Two years earlier, Rossi, the high-priced scorer for Lanerossi Vincenza, had been found guilty of participating in a fixed-odds betting scandal while on loan to the club Perugia. Perugia tied 2–2 in a match at Avellino, with Rossi scoring two goals. It was a fix. Italian fans adopted the old American saying about Chicago White Sox Shoeless Joe Jackson for their own use: "Say it ain't so, Paolo."

Rossi had signed a $4.8 million contract with Lanerossi Vincenza back in 1978; an outrageous sum in those days, and a deal that led to the resignation of the president of the Italian League in protest.

**THE ELUSIVE ROSSI WAS EVERYWHERE—
AND, AT THE SAME TIME, NOWHERE.**

Rossi had afforded himself well at the 1978 World Cup in Argentina. But now, after the scandal, all seemed lost.

A tribunal in Milan handed down a three-year suspension, later reduced to a lenient (and convenient) two years. This one-year reduction proved critical for Rossi, and for Italy. He joined Juventus just before the 1982 World Cup, then went on to become the toast of Spain in Italy's championship.

After a slow start—Rossi was, after all, a bit rusty from his suspension—he awoke with a hat trick during a second-round 3–2 victory against Brazil. He scored five minutes into the match on a header, scored again off an interception, and scored a third goal in the seventy-fifth minute off a flawed clearing attempt. Against Poland in the semifinal, Rossi scored at the twenty-two-minute mark, and again on a header in the seventy-third minute for a 2–0 victory. In the final against Germany, Rossi scored the first goal on yet another header, dashing toward the goal mouth from the left and beating Toni Schumacher. Then, for good measure, he set up Italy's second goal. The elusive Rossi was everywhere—and, at the same time, nowhere.

Reinstated as a national hero, Rossi continued his soccer career at home. But injuries slowed him to the point where he was virtually useless to the 1986 World Cup team and to coach Enzo Bearzot.

Toto Schillaci celebrates another Italian goal.

SALVATORE SCHILLACI

SALVATORE "TOTO" SCHILLACI BECAME A WONDERFUL, HOME-GROWN story as the 1990 World Cup was played out before the passionate Italian fans.

A scrappy attacker for Juventus of Turin, Schillaci barely made the national team and came on as a second-half replacement in the opening match against Austria. He scored the only goal of that game on an opportunistic headball. Schillaci was now a starter. Toto-mania had begun. By the end of play, the dark Sicilian with the receding hairline had amassed a tournament-high six goals and won the Golden Boot as the most valuable player of the tournament.

It was an honor Schillaci deserved. Here was a player with a nose for the ball, and the rebound, who was not too lazy to chase either one down himself. Of his six goals, three were true beauties. His gorgeous leaping, looping goal against Uruguay was perhaps the score of the Cup.

"His have been beautiful goals, and game-winners," Italy coach Azeglio Vicini said. "We are fortunate to have a player who is playing at the top of his game."

Schillaci, a grade-school dropout and one-time petty thief, suddenly found himself a spokesman for his team and his country. When Diego Maradona said Italy was divided, North against South, it was Schillaci who eloquently defended his sometimes unworthy nation. "Our quest for the Cup this month has been a symbol against racism in Italy," Schillaci said.

Unfortunately, about the time Schillaci said this, a comedian on national television predicted that the final would be Cameroon against Italy. "Schillaci could play for either team," the comedian said, referring to Schillaci's dark pigmentation. Everyone in the Florence studio audience laughed.

Still, Schillaci was on T-shirts, and on the cover of every newspaper and magazine in the country. He asked for a contract extension with Juventus, and was promised he would get it. While the stock of fellow attacker Gianni Vialli had plummeted, Schillaci's had leaped above all. Italia '90 was his.

Toni Schumacher

OF ALL THE WORLD CUP STARS LISTED IN THIS SECTION, HARALD "Toni" Schumacher is perhaps the least athletically talented. And yet, through two World Cup finals in 1982 and 1986, this dogged goaltender was the heart and soul of the West Germans. He was the alter ego of Karl-Heinz Rummenigge, and he flaunted his emotions on the field in a way that seemed more South American or Italian than German.

Schumacher's reputation, both as a prescient netminder and an overaggressive bully, were both assured in the dramatic semifinal against France in 1982. Then, at age twenty-eight, he was at the top of his arrogant game. On one play, he rushed from his net and slammed French defender Patrick Battiston with his forearm, breaking Battiston's jaw and knocking out several teeth. Later, in a

Toni Schumacher, the goalie you love to hate, celebrates a 1986 victory over Scotland.

ON ONE PLAY, HE RUSHED FROM HIS NET AND SLAMMED FRENCH DEFENDER PATRICK BATTISTON WITH HIS FOREARM, BREAKING BATTISTON'S JAW AND KNOCKING OUT SEVERAL TEETH.

shootout tie-breaker, Schumacher made consecutive saves on penalty kicks from Didier Six and Maxine Bossis to clinch victory for the Germans.

Schumacher's hands are not the surest, and he has been criticized for yielding too many rebounds. But his instincts and his aggression make up for all other shortcomings. In two World Cups, the slim, blond Schumacher gave up just over one goal per game. He also found time for several screaming matches with his teammates and coaches, including German institutions Rummenigge and Franz Beckenbauer.

"I always say what I think, irrespective of whether it suits me or not," Schumacher said.

Schumacher always preferred to stay near home, playing for German club teams. And yet, he did not always make friends among the German players. He remained so competitive during practices, he was known to injure teammates. For Schumacher it was all in a day's work.

TOMAS SKUHRAVY

THERE WERE TIMES IN 1990 WHEN IT APPEARED TOMAS SKUHRAVY would be swept away by the political tide of events in Czechoslovakia. The attacking constancy of the lanky striker was simply not headline news in a country where social change had become an obsession.

Some of the upheaval directly affected the Czech team. Stars Lubos Kubik and Ivo Knoflicek returned to the national team following a year-long defection, stealing all the pre-tournament publicity from Skuhravy. Then the 1990 World Cup started, and Skuhravy was once again the center of attention.

In the first match against the United States, the Sparta Prague forward scored two goals in a 5–1 rout. In a second-round victory over Costa Rica, Skuhravy added three more. Altogether, he scored five goals, the second highest at the World Cup. He had scored four other goals in qualification matches leading to Italy, no easy road past Portugal.

"I dedicate all my goals to Vaclav Havel, and the Civic Forum," the idealistic patriot, Skuhravy, said. "We have many things on our minds in Czechoslovakia, and soccer is only one of them."

Skuhravy's style was hardly renaissance soccer. A bit gawky, he depended desperately on the ability of his Czech teammates to lob crosses or dead-ball sets high to his head. Skuhravy had the uncanny ability to lurch forward at the correct moment, propelling the ball with his forehead past even the best-prepared goalies. Unfortunately, against the West Germans in the quarterfinals, Skuhravy's teammates lost their ability to service his brow, and he became just another awkward, futile attacker. Skuhravy turned twenty-five the day after the 1990 World Cup final, and probably will have one more go at the next qualifying run.

Have head, will travel. Tomas Skuhravy's forehead never met a ball it didn't like. Here, against Costa Rica, he scores one of his three goals in a 1990 second-round match.

GUILLERMO STABILE

His ability to penetrate through packed penalty boxes had forever earned him the nickname "El Enfiltrador" (the Infiltrator).

THE ARGENTINIAN STRIKER GUILLERMO STABILE MIGHT NEVER HAVE had his chance to score eight goals in the inaugural World Cup tournament of 1930 had he not been pressed into service for his country's second match by strange circumstance.

In these early days, when priorities were a bit more sensible, Argentina forward Manuel Ferreira decided to skip Argentina's match in order to take his university exam. Stabile replaced Ferreira, scored three goals against Mexico, and never sat again, even after Ferreira returned from his exam. Stabile scored two against Chile, and two against the United States in a semifinal victory.

Stabile then scored an eighth goal, albeit a controversial one, in Argentina's 4–2 loss in the final to Uruguay. In the thirty-fifth minute, Stabile's goal gave Argentina a 2–1 lead it would carry into the halftime locker room. Uruguay argued, vociferously, that Stabile had wandered offside on the play. In the end, Stabile's ambush of the 1930 World Cup fell two goals shy of a championship. But his ability to penetrate through packed penalty boxes had forever earned him the nickname "El Enfiltrador" (The Infiltrator).

Later, a national hero for his exploits in Uruguay, Stabile assumed the reins of Argentina's national team as coach. But Argentina would not play in the World Cup in France in 1938, and then the war would come. Stabile never returned to the tournament that had treated him so well.

DINO ZOFF

DINO ZOFF WORKED LONG AND HARD TO GET TO THE WORLD CUP. Passed over in 1966 and 1970 by the Italian Federation, he finally convinced officials of his competency with an unequaled string of shutout goaltending.

Zoff played more than ten straight international matches for Italy without giving up a goal, a world record of 1,143 minutes that still stands. Undoubtedly, some of the credit for this achievement must go to Italy's conservative *catenaccio* style. But Zoff, too, was a perfectionist. He showed great technical skill, acrobatics, and bravery.

Zoff's shutout streak ended in his first World Cup match, in 1974 at West Germany, when Haiti scored a goal in the second half. He would not taste champagne until 1982 in Rome, where the forty-year-old captain led host Italy to its third World Cup title. By this time, Zoff was a bit slow to leave his mark on the crossing pass, but he was still a master of the angles.

Zoff was a leader by example, an amiable man who urged on his defenders without chiding them. This patience might have been a product of his long climb to the top. He spent six years getting to Naples, then another five years before he was offered a contract, in 1972, by Juventus. He made outstanding saves against Mario Kempes and Passarella during a 1–0 win over Argentina in the 1978 World Cup, and set the battle cry for a big victory over France: "We wanted to show them we weren't the imbeciles they took us for," Zoff said.

With inspiring words like those, it was not surprising that Zoff was named captain and carried off the field by his teammates after Italy's World Cup triumph in 1982. It was a wonderful farewell party for Zoff, who would finally be too old, at forty-four, to anchor the *catenaccio* trap in 1986.

Not an inch farther: Talkative Dino Zoff carries on a conversation with a soccer ball, delivered by Argentine in 1982. It did not cross the line.

Moore, a graceful 6-foot (1.8-m) blond from East London, developed his special defensive left-wing-halfback style at West Ham United under coach Ron Greenwood. He made his first World Cup appearance at Chile in 1962, and was named captain of England and later player of the tournament in the 1966 World Cup on home ground. An aggressive passer and tackler, Moore took chances and created them. He assisted Geoff Hurst on two of his goals in the final against Germany in 1966, then played brilliantly in defeat against Pelé and Brazil in 1970.

"I consider him the finest defenseman in the world," Pelé said later. "The shirt he wore against Brazil during the World Cup is a prized possession in my collection at home."

Moore had his share of problems off the field, it seemed, but they were never carried onto the pitch, where he was cool, calm, and deadly. In 1964, on tour with the national team, Moore broke curfew in New York and greatly angered coach Alf Ramsey. It took years, and a World Cup title, for the two to patch things up. In November 1970, Moore and three other West Ham players went out drinking on the eve of a match at Blackpool; West Ham lost the match 4-0. Moore was fined and suspended for five weeks.

Finally, in July 1978, after 108 appearances with the national team, Moore went to that great burial ground of aging soccer stars, the North American Soccer League, playing briefly with the Seattle Sounders at age thirty-seven. He had earned the victory lap.

Bobby Moore, the captain, respectfully takes the Cup from Queen Elizabeth.

GERD MULLER

A familiar sight: Record-scorer Gerd Muller racing a goalie for the ball in the penalty box. This time, it's against Yugoslavia.

HIS CAREER FOURTEEN WORLD CUP GOALS REMAIN AN ALL-TIME RECORD.

THE TALE OF GERD MULLER, WEST GERMANY'S CHUNKY LITTLE center-forward, is as remarkable as the rags-to-riches stories of Pelé or Eusebio.

Born in the isolated Bavarian village of Zinsen in 1945, Muller had a tough time finding soccer matches worthy of his skills. Muller's father died when he was young, and the boy dropped out of school at age fifteen to become an apprentice weaver and part-time soccer player. Playing with borrowed boots, Muller scored two goals in a tryout with local club TSV Nordlingen and was signed immediately.

With his thick legs and low center of gravity, the 5-foot, 8-inch (1.7 m) Muller was nicknamed "Dicker," or "Fatty." When he was first recruited by Bayern Munich (because of forty-six goals in two seasons with Nordlingen), coach Tchik Cajkovski is said to have asked his scout, "Do you want me to put a bear among my race horses?"

Soon, there were no more questions. Bayern won the European Cup with Muller in 1966 and 1967, when Muller tallied twenty-eight goals. Muller scored nine goals in World Cup qualifiers leading up to Mexico in 1970, then scored ten goals in the World Cup itself. He was named European Footballer of the Year in 1971. He scored forty goals for Bayern in 1972. In 1974, he netted four more goals, including the match-winner in the final against Holland. His career fourteen World Cup goals remain an all-time record.

Muller never demonstrated the flair of a Pelé or the elegance of a Beckenbauer, but he was a bullish player with great power. His ability to poach goals, and to shed defenders by his sheer power, earned him the new, more dignified nickname "King of the Penalty Box." He scored 365 goals in 427 Bundesliga games, then went overseas for three seasons in the mid-1970s and scored thirty-eight

The Countries

Each nation is stamped with a particular soccer style, be it imposed by a tyrannical coach or mystically, genetically coded into every player's trap and dribble. You don't need uniforms to tell the Italians from the Dutch. Why can't the Americans, an enormous nation now saturated by youth leagues, find a scorer? Why are the Germans so fit, the English so rough, the Brazilians so artistic?

What decides tempo? Why do the South Americans play slow, slow, fast? The Europeans fast, fast, fast? There are no answers, of course. But this clash of divergent styles is what makes watching a World Cup match a treat. Here are some of the nations that collectively have helped to define World Cup competition while marching distinctly to their own drummers.

ARGENTINA

Not a great moment for Argentine soccer: Cameroon stalks Diego Maradona during the 1990 World Cup opener, holding the great scorer scoreless and upsetting Argentina, 1–0, in Milan.

WHATEVER ELSE HAS GONE WRONG IN ARGENTINA OVER THE PAST twelve years—humiliation in war, governmental ineptitude, economic hardship—soccer has been a great elixir for the public. Argentina might have lost the 1982 Falklands War, but some countrymen honestly believed a 2–1 victory over England in the 1986 World Cup was far more important.

With this kind of fanaticism, it is not surprising that great coaching controversies are an obsession here. Until coach Carlos Bilardo won the World Cup in 1986, he was constantly harangued about why he did not do things the way his predecessor, Cesar Luis Menotta, did in winning the World Cup in 1978. These same rooters had dubbed Menotta "El Loco" (The Crazy One) before he won the World Cup in 1978.

No matter who coaches Argentina (Bilardo was just a bit more conservative and defensive-oriented than Menotta), he will have to rely on the strong, individualistic play of a handful of superstars. Argentina will never be systematized like England or West Germany. Its top players often perform for big money overseas in Europe until World Cup time, so there is no great synthesis or unity in the National Team.

Instead, with players like the great Diego Maradona, Argentina relies on the classic South American style: bunching around the ball on offense, with soft, one-touch passing. The occasional dart downfield has been known to happen, but usually a more artistic approach is preferred until the ball is in the opponent's penalty box. Then, it is hoped, a player like Maradona can finish the play with a nifty dribble and shot.

When Argentina has had the requisite number of stars, this ad-lib style has worked well enough to win two championships. It nearly worked again in 1990, when Argentina survived to the final on sheer grit, luck, and some very naughty tackles. But with four starters suspended in the final against West Germany, from a group that was not particularly deep or creative from the start, the Argentines and Maradona went down ugly, 1–0. Bilardo, possibly the coach of the tournament, was forced to make excuses for his team to a furiously committed nation.

BELGIUM

UNTIL THE 1980s, BELGIUM HAD INSCRIBED A LONG, BUT NOT particularly proud, soccer history. The "Red Devils" were part of the very first World Cup in 1930, but lost badly to the United States. They lost again in 1934, 1938, and 1954, before finally winning their first match in 1970 at Mexico.

Even then, there was disappointment. Entering the tournament as one of the favorites, infighting broke out among the squad over, of all things, soccer shoes. Adidas and Puma had divided the Belgians into warring capitalistic factions, with a third group of players jealous because it had been courted by neither manufacturer. Perhaps because of this nonsense, Belgium wasted the strong coaching efforts of Raymond Goethals and the midfield play of Odilon Polleunis. It was eliminated quite easily, 1–0, by host country Mexico.

Finally, in 1982, when little was expected of it in Spain, Belgium opened the tournament with a stunning 1–0 win over defending champion Argentina. Riding the foot of former European scoring champ Ervin Vandenbergh and his passing mate Alex Czerniatynski, the Belgians made it to the second round where they then lost.

In 1986, again utilizing the well-designed forward passing of coach Guy Thys, Belgium surpassed expectations by reaching the semifinals. It was not an easily explained journey, because the Belgians lacked star material everywhere but in goal (Jean-Marie Pfaff). Yet, they defeated the favored Soviets 4–3 in overtime, then defeated Spain on penalty kicks in the quarterfinal.

As one Belgian partisan was quoted as saying in Brussels, "I've never seen anything like this. Apart from when Belgium was liberated at the end of World War II, there hasn't been anything to cheer about."

The Belgians again put on a nice show in 1990, playing some of the most aggressive, open soccer in Italy. Their 3–1 victory over Uruguay was superb; their overtime loss to England in the second round was heartbreaking. In twenty-four-year-old Vincenzo Scifo, the Red Devils boasted perhaps the most artistic upstart of the tournament.

Vincenzo Scifo is the soul of the Belgian attack.

© Allsport

BRAZIL

Brazil, World Cup champions of 1958. The names were as interesting as the team's style: Didi, Vava, Garrincha, and Mario Lobo Zagalo.

THROUGH THREE TITLES...AND A SEEMINGLY ENDLESS STREAM OF SUPERSTARS, BRAZIL HAS BEEN THE CROWN JEWEL OF THE WORLD CUP.

TO A BRAZILIAN PLAYER, SOCCER OUGHT TO BE A PRIVATE CANVAS upon which to dash off impressionistic patterns and dazzling rushes. At its best, there is nothing quite as exhilarating as Brazilian soccer, with four attackers going headlong for the goal; at its worst, there is nothing quite as futile and inherently selfish.

Fortunately, the world has been treated more to the wonderful than to the dreadful. Through three titles (in 1958, 1962, and 1970) and a seemingly endless stream of superstars, Brazil has been the crown jewel of the World Cup, in which it has appeared a record thirteen times.

Historically, coaches Vincente Feola and Zeze Moreira were intelligent enough to step out of the way and let players like Garrincha, Pelé, Edinho, Socrates, and Roberto Rivellino create magic with their feet, not with a restrictive system. More recently, at the 1990 Cup, Sebastiao Lazaroni tried to install a more conservative European sweeper system, with predictably disastrous results: Brazil was first an artistic flop, then a 1–0 loser to inferior Argentina in the second round. Lazaroni was chased out of Brazil upon his return, leaving immediately to coach in Florence, Italy.

The classic Brazilian style is the South American model, to the extreme. Defense is played with a deep zone. Short passing and irregular pace are the rule on offense. Brazil lulls opponents with its slow, soft-touch passing at midfield, then suddenly turns up the throttle and heads toward the goal. Once in the penalty box, phenomenal ball control and a flair for showmanship have made Brazilian strikers the most dangerous in the game. It is no coincidence that the originator of the scissors kick was a Brazilian, Leonidas, a center forward on the national side in the 1930s.

This style of play—threatened not only by the Lazaronis, but by the exposure of homegrown stars to European club play—allows the Brazilians to "coast" for entire portions of matches, conserving their energy for important moments in important matches. This strategy is not foolproof, however. In recent Cups, European sides have flustered the Brazilians with hard tackling at midfield, blunting the offense. The goaltending has been less than adequate. And occasionally, a coach like Continho (circa 1978) or Lazaroni comes around and tries to remake Brazil into a more European image. This inevitably means disaster, and is not nearly as pleasing as Pelé on the dribble, green-and-yellow uniform flashing through crowds of defenders, dancing to the samba chants of the Brazilian supporters in the stands. One must always remember that soccer is religion in Brazil, and that when that nation won the World Cup for a third time in 1970, President Emilio Garrastazu Medici, a somber army general, declared a two-day holiday and joined a crowd dancing in the street.

CANADA

IT IS PROBABLY OF LITTLE CONSOLATION TO CANADIAN SOCCER FANS, but if nothing else, their country's national team has had remarkable success against its southern neighbor, the United States.

Canada has effectively been knocking the United States out of World Cup qualifying rounds since 1958, when it whipped the Americans 5–1 and 3–2 in regional competition. Unfortunately, this has not always assured success against other, smaller Central American nations in the CONCACAF grouping. Canada suffered an embarrassing preliminary round knockout by Guatemala in the 1990 qualification process, even before it could get to its personal patsy, the United States.

Canada qualified for the final round of the World Cup only once in its history, in 1986. Its problems in Mexico, however, were indicative of wholesale troubles throughout the program. First, Canadian Soccer Association president Jim Fleming had difficulty obtaining his best players from a professional indoor soccer league (the Major Indoor Soccer League—MISL). Then, with limited practice time and no effective strikers, the Canadians were shut out three times: by Hungary, France, and the Soviet Union.

The Canadian style is similar to the American style, which is, in the first place, a sloppy version of the English and German models. It is marked by close, hard tackling, much running, and very little finesse inside the penalty box. Considering the cold climate and geographical problems facing the Canadian organizers, it will be difficult to forge a stronger soccer identity in the future. A financial commitment to the top players—similar to the plan in effect in the United States—could help. Canadians can hope that the proximity of the 1994 World Cup will spark fresh interest all around.

*CANADA QUALIFIED FOR THE FINAL ROUND OF THE WORLD CUP ONLY ONCE IN ITS HISTORY, IN **1986**.*

CZECHOSLOVAKIA

AFTER THREE DECADES OF EXCELLENCE AND TWO WORLD CUP FINALS, Czech soccer came upon very hard times beginning in 1966 and only recently has shown some sparks of recovery—highlighted by a quarterfinal appearance at the 1990 World Cup.

The rigid, authoritarian government imposed by the Russians in 1968, and ending with the fall of Communism in eastern Europe in 1989, brought with it the standard Eastern bloc emphasis on specialized Olympic events (gymnastics, shooting, ski jumping), which so easily produce quick results and medals. Ice hockey, another program receiving great state attention and funding, began attracting many of the nation's top young athletes, particularly those seeking more physical outlets. The club teams remained mired in a slow, short passing game of *ceske ulicka*, or "street soccer." Czech spectators, recognizing the drop in quality, lost interest in soccer and attendance fell dramatically.

All of these problems might have been solved by the right player or the right coach, but the Czechs have been unable to discover either precious commodity since the glory years of 1934 and 1962. Back then, it seemed, tactical geniuses and sure-handed goaltenders grew on the linden trees of Prague. But Austrian-born Rudolf Vytlacil, the innovative coach who led the Czechs to an incredible string of upsets in 1962 at Chile, left to coach Bulgaria and nobody

Not even another acrobatic goalie can rescue the Czechs in this 1954 match against Uruguay. Raiman made the save, but Czechoslovakia fell, 2–0.

furthered his bold ideas or selection methods. And there will never be another Frantisek Planicka, the brilliant netminder who made 1934 possible.

When the Czechs play at their best, they mix the strong-minded defensive discipline of the Eastern European nations with a dash of individual offensive creativity that might almost be termed South American—or at least, Italian. In the seventies, coach Vaclav Jezek attempted—with some success—to bring a new system of "block movement" to the national team, in which the defense advanced *en masse* on attack. But Jezek had more setbacks than halfbacks, and inevitably failed.

When they are at their worst, the Czechs are at their dullest, with a predictable offense as easily countered as that of Bulgaria or Russia. The slow, skilled style that was once good enough for Jozef Masopust and Ladislav Novak is often not good enough today.

In 1990, the Czechs came to Italy with a different idea. Their lineup was exceptionally tall, filled with headball and dead-ball specialists. While they lacked team speed, they posed some unsolvable problems for weaker teams. They scored five goals against the Americans, four against the Costa Ricans, but finally fell 1–0 to West Germany, the eventual champions.

DENMARK

TINY DENMARK, WITHOUT A SUBSTANTIAL PROFESSIONAL LEAGUE OF its own, historically has exported its most talented players to other European nations, much like its South American counterpart, Uruguay. This has made it virtually impossible for Danish coaches to produce a cohesive national team, and Denmark failed to qualify for any World Cup competition until 1986 in Mexico.

Talent, however, can be irrepressible. The generation of Danish players that finally made it to Mexico impacted greatly on the festivities, quickly becoming a crowd favorite with its wide-open style. Forwards Preben Elkjaer-Larsen and Michael Laudrup—both of whom were recalled from Italian pro clubs—joined veterans Morten Olsen and Jesper Olsen to produce some amazing offensive thrusts, and outlandish scores.

In that coming-out party, Denmark routed physical Uruguay 6–1 and defeated the eventual winners, West Germany, 2–0. The Danes' Achilles' heel turned out to be the same Spanish team that had defeated it in the 1984 European Championships. When Denmark fell apart, it did so with a cacophonous clang. Leading 1–0, it was eventually routed by Spain 5–1.

Experts debated the exact meaning of this one-match debacle, and eventually dismissed it as an unfortunate, uncharacteristic lapse. But after a few more years of successes, the Danes lost a shocking 3–1 qualifying finale to Romania in November 1989, and missed the World Cup in Italy. It would help if players like Elkjaer and Laudrup could play together more often, instead of against each other on teams like Juventus and Verona. But with a total land area .6 percent as large as the continental United States, and with a population of just 5.1 million (and falling!), Denmark appears doomed to remain a soccer exporter.

ENGLAND

On the verge: Sir Alf Ramsey, England's legendary soccer coach, is just days away from the start of the 1966 World Cup—and England's moment of triumph.

ENGLAND IS GENERALLY CREDITED WITH BEING THE FATHER OF modern soccer, but its play in World Cup competition has spawned just one champion. Except for 1966, when legendary coach Alf Ramsey successfully defended the homefield advantage with his 4–3–3 formation and sturdy midfield play, England's international results have been far too erratic.

Banished from international club play since the 1985 Heysel Stadium soccer riots because of its violent hooligan supporters, few people expected much from England at Italia '90. And yet, England displayed some hard, direct soccer that carried it all the way to a shootout defeat in a semifinal loss to the eventual champion, West Germany. Not only was Bobby Robson's team fit and competitive, it was also promising. Young Paul Gascoigne took over where injured captain Bryan Robson left off, engineering dangerous drives from midfield and the wing.

"We're isolated," Bobby Robson said. "But despite the lack of education, our game hasn't gone that far backward at all.

"We get talked about as medieval football. I hope those people kicked the bucket now."

England, and retiring Robson, will always face criticism for the country's inflexible soccer style, an ugly model abandoned by all but the British empire and its former North American colonies. English soccer is about tight, man-to-man marking on defense; about long, high passes and goaltender punts; and about offensive thrusts along the flank, climaxed with deep crossing passes. This all requires tremendous energy and non-stop running, which is quite difficult to sustain throughout a month-long tournament in summer temperatures. It is also a predictable style easy to defend against, once opponents get the hang of it. Sometimes, it seems, the English have not evolved at all since Arsenal coach Herbert Chapman invented the basic W.M. formation between world wars.

Still, the style is competitive, more so now that the international ban has been lifted on all but Liverpool. In any case, the English will always have 1966, a whirlwind ride to the championship played out before a fanatic but civil audience at Wembley. Ramsey, a former fullback with a midfielder's vision during his playing days at Tottenham Hotspur, customized the push-and-run tactics he learned from mentor Arthur Rowe. He applied them to a uniquely talented group of English players, led by innovators Bobby Moore and Bobby Charlton. For once, everything fell in place, including an overtime goal against West Germany in the final that may or may not have crossed the goal line.

England gained confidence in this 0–0 tie with Holland, then advanced to the semifinals of the 1990 World Cup.

© Allsport

FRANCE

Michel Platini's daring ingenuity is the essence of French football flair.

ALTHOUGH FRANCE IS INDISPUTABLY LOCATED IN EUROPE, ITS soccer heart beats in South America. Unlike the European sides who rely on harsh tackling and heavy breathing, the French players go about their business with a certain *joie de vivre* and a flair for the dramatic.

For many years, frail France suffered one indignant setback after another. The national team became known as a group that easily fell apart on the road when pressured or fouled. But in 1976, Michel Hidalgo became coach when a group of talented midfielders were coming into their own, and when the financial resources were discovered to keep these players in France. The combination was explosive, Hidalgo harnessing this creative energy and putting his own systematic stamp on Les Bleus (The Blues).

In 1982 at Spain, the dazzling French team led 3-1 in overtime of the semifinal against West Germany before eventually losing in a shootout. In 1986, new coach Henri Michel took a similar team, using many of Hidalgo's theories, into the semis again. This time, emotionally exhausted by a brilliant victory over soccer soul sister Brazil, the French were easier prey for the Germans, losing 2-0.

Historically, the French have had magicians at midfield, but ordinary mortals at the forward positions. This distinction was never clearer than when the French were at their best, with wizard Michel Platini, the chain-smoking genius, and Alain Giresse creating chances from the rear that were often botched or ignored near the goal mouth. When these masters grew old, the French threat abated and the team failed to qualify for Italy in 1990.

HUNGARY

HUNGARY'S NATIONAL TEAM ROSE FROM THE ASHES OF WORLD WAR II and crashed with the revolution. Its steep ascent and equally sharp descent spanned all of four years, and the country has suffered three decades of soccer mediocrity ever since. Since 1954, Hungary has survived to the quarterfinals of the World Cup only twice, the last time in 1966. On those few occasions it has shown promise, but ill-timed injuries have sabotaged success.

But there will always be the early fifties for Hungary, when it ruled soccer with players like Ferenc Puskas, Sandor Kocsis, Nandor Hidegkuti, and Josef Bozsik. Hungarian coach Gyula Mandi and deputy minister of sport Gustav Sebes made certain this uniquely talented group of athletes had all the advantages a totalitarian state could offer: Nearly all the players practiced together and played together for Honved, the army team.

At their peak right before the 1954 World Cup in Switzerland, the Hungarians came very close to inventing a "total soccer" model used twenty years later by the Dutch. The players quickly changed field positions, catching passes on the run. Collectively, they made Mandi appear a genius.

The course of human events had other things in store, however. The Honved team was on tour when the Russians crushed the 1956 revolution, and most of the top players defected. Puskas and Kocsis eventually went to Spain. By the 1958 World Cup in Sweden, Sebes reportedly was led to comment, "I have never seen a Hungarian team in such a deplorable physical condition and nervous state."

Although there have been some strong Hungarian forwards since then—Tibor Nyilasi, for example, in the late seventies and early eighties—there has never been another Puskas, or another 1954.

Before their loss in the 1954 final, Hungary lost to Italy, 4–2, in the 1938 World Cup final.

ITALY

The little Sicilian, Toto Schillaci, with another all-out dash for the goal—this time against Uruguay in the second round of Italia '90. Schillaci finished with six goals, and the Golden Boot.

An Italian fan proudly displays a picture of his—and all of Italy's—hero, Paolo Rossi, in the 1982 World Cup.

IT IS A SEEMING CONTRADICTION THAT HAS WORKED SO WELL for the resilient Italians: iron-willed coaches demanding discipline from non-conformist players.

This formula has resulted in three World Cups for Italy, and two of the strongest coaching personalities to ever glare from the sidelines: Vittorio Pozzo and Enzo Bearzot. Pozzo was responsible for Italy's first two World Cups in 1934 and 1938. He was a shrewd motivator who constantly played mind games with his players, and who once called himself "King, with a strong hand. If I let them make mistakes, I lose my authority." Pozzo modeled the Italian team after English football, yet he had the sense to build in some necessary alterations allowing for the Italians' inherent need for self-expression on offense.

Bearzot, now sixty-three, coached the Italian national team to the 1982 championship, with the help of star Paolo Rossi. Yet Bearzot would never defer to Rossi, or anybody else. "I believe in the group, the family," he said. "They must have absolute compatibility."

The Azzurri (The Blues) and most professional teams in Italy have relied heavily on the *catenaccio* system, "the great chain," since its invention in the late fifties by Helenio Herrera, an assistant to head coach Giannino Ferrari and later, himself, head coach of Spain. In this set, seven players retreat to mark closely, man-to-man, in the defensive third of the field. Four defenders pack the penalty box. This formation leaves the wings open, keying instead on those who might get the crosses. It makes penetration extremely difficult, unless it is done by the wings themselves.

This sort of pre-programmed conservatism belies the spirituality of this team, of its attack, and of its followers. In 1990, the safety-first doctrine might have cost talented Italy a fourth title. Coach Azeglio Vicini allowed the Italians to move too comfortably to a five-back formation, protecting a 1–0 lead against Argentina in the second half of a semifinal. The result was a single mistake by goalie Walter Zenga, an eventual shootout defeat, and many recriminations by the host Italians about Vicini's uninspired leadership.

In Italy, as the 1990 World Cup demonstrated, there is nothing quite as transcendent as soccer.

MEXICO

RECENTLY, THE MEXICAN SOCCER ASSOCIATION HAS BEEN IN THE midst of reorganization, rocked by the scandal that knocked this nation out of the 1990 World Cup competition. FIFA banned Mexico from Italy for using overaged players in an international under-twenty competition, an infraction that offered few benefits and created horrible repercussions.

Until 1990, FIFA traditionally had been most charitable to Mexican soccer. FIFA placed Mexico in the relatively weak CONCACAF region, where it should have been assured of a World Cup qualifying spot every four years (although it failed in 1982). And Mexico is one of only two nations to have been awarded the World Cup site twice, an advantage that has turned other hosts into champions.

Yet despite these historic boosts, the Mexicans have yet to make a real impact on world soccer. In both 1970 and 1986, when it played host, Mexico survived to the quarterfinals. Other than that, there have been only early-round eliminations, and the Mexican style remains a poor man's version of the classic South American soft-touch, high-skill model.

There is much debate within Mexico, as one can imagine, about the team's lackluster results. In the mid-1980s, Mexico's professional league owners made nearly all the country's top players available for practice and international exhibitions in preparation for the 1986 World Cup. This would have seemed to be a tremendous edge, and yet Enrique Borja, a star from the 1970s, saw problems with it. "When you know the other team members too well,

Mexican goalie Pablo Larios heads off a goal in a 1986 World Cup match against Paraguay.

© David Cannon/Allsport

then other kinds of problems might begin to surface," he predicted before the World Cup.

The Mexicans' renowned infighting doubled when superstar Hugo Sanchez returned from Spain, then missed a crucial penalty kick in the first round against Paraguay. West Germany eventually proved too much for the Mexicans, and for camp counselor/coach Bora Milutinovic.

THE NETHERLANDS

The two captains—Franz Beckenbauer of West Germany and Johann Cruyff of the Netherlands—take a rest during the 1974 World Cup final. Cruyff's team was better, but it lost.

IT IS IMPOSSIBLE TO CONSIDER HOLLAND'S SPOTTY SOCCER HISTORY without focusing on the glorious seventies. During a half-decade and two World Cups, the Dutch redefined the sport in an exciting way—even if the hype of total soccer unfairly overshadowed the sheer individual talents of players like Johann Cruyff, Johan Neeskens, and Rob Resenbrink.

The concept of total soccer was liberating from the start. Based on a "reactive" model fashioned by Ajax manager Rinus Michels, players were freed from the bonds of positional play and asked to take part in all facets of the game. Attackers became aggressive tacklers when opponents controlled the ball. Defenders became offensive playmakers, rushing to open spots on the field to gather in and redistribute the ball on the run.

This high-scoring style, fitted perfectly to Cruyff's remarkable generation, won three successive European Cups in 1971, 1972, and 1973. It should have won two World Cups, in 1974 and 1978, but fell just short to host countries West Germany and Argentina.

Since that time, Holland has continued to utilize this crowd-pleasing style, but with varying degrees of success. The group in the seventies had played together for years in Holland's pro leagues. It dispersed soon after 1978, and the same sort of comradeship, passing touch, and overall chemistry were difficult to forge. There was also an all-too-evident drop-off in talent, as Holland failed to qualify for World Cup play in 1982 or 1986.

A resurrection followed, thankfully. The spirit of Cruyff et al. pulsated again through the Netherlands' 1988 European Cup title run, with vibrant attackers like Ruud Gullit, Fank Rijkaard, and Marco Van Basten, all of whom exported their league soccer to

Milan. The men in bright orange shirts were a dangerous side again, and always an entertaining one. They qualified for Italy in 1990 ahead of West Germany in their group. But Gullit's injuries, Van Basten's fatigue, and the team's inability to mesh for unpopular coach Leo Beenhakker (the players wanted Johann Cruyff) in a short period led to a quick second-round departure in a rousing 2–1 loss to Germany.

POLAND

POLAND WENT THIRTY-SIX YEARS WITHOUT QUALIFYING FOR THE World Cup. When it finally returned in 1974, it did so with a vengeance. Over the next eight years—and three World Cups—Poland had the best record of all nations, advancing to the second round three times and finishing in third place twice. By 1986, it seemed some of that momentum had faded, and an eye-opening 4–0 loss to Brazil in the second round at Mexico told the nation's soccer officials it was time to retool their passing game with younger, faster players. That new team, still learning and growing, failed to qualify for Italy in 1990.

The sixteen-year renaissance began in 1970 with the success of showcase club Gornik, which advanced to the European Cup Winners Cup final behind the play of inside-forward Wlodzimierz Lubanski. With the help of midfielder Kazimierz Deyna and a crop of talented "total soccer" players, Poland won the gold medal at the 1972 Olympics in Munich, West Germany. With this new-found success came financial and spectator backing. The country's first division expanded from fourteen to sixteen clubs by 1973, setting the stage for some artistic World Cup triumphs.

The Polish style in those glory years is best described as a counter-attacking set, working best against teams that overextend themselves on offense, but leaves them vulnerable in the rear. Polish coach Antoni Piechniczek, an amiable and humble man, was constantly reminding journalists in 1982, even in victory, how hapless his team was against more conservative opponents.

"I fear the Italians very much," he said before a 2–0 semifinal defeat to them in Madrid. "I would rather play Brazil."

As it was, that match against eventual champion Italy probably

The start of the renaissance: Poland, in the 1974 World Cup, against Brazil. Over the next decade, the Poles were a top soccer power.

represented Poland's best chance for a World Cup title. But top-scoring midfielder Zbigniew Boniek was sitting out a one-game suspension he incurred for rough play during another holy war against the Soviet Union. Traditionally—before *perestroika*, democratic elections, and Gorbachev—the Poles saved their most inspired, emotional efforts for the Russians. At Barcelona in 1982, the Poles played the Soviets to a 0–0 tie that eliminated the Russians, as fans chanted, "Polska, Polska."

After the tournament, more than half of the six hundred Polish tourists in Spain sought asylum in the West. Unlike most fans, the Poles have always taken their politics as seriously as their soccer. And, like the other communist countries in Eastern Europe, it is still unclear how the dramatic and exciting political changes will affect the national teams.

SCOTLAND

Scotland survived France in 1989 to qualify for the 1990 World Cup, but failed to advance, again, to the second round.

SCOTLAND IS NO STRANGER TO THE WORLD CUP, AND TO WORLD CUP disappointment. Dating back to appearances in 1954 and 1958, it has never survived the first round, much to the disappointment of its wonderfully colorful supporters, the Plaid Army.

Despite this remarkable record of futility, Scotland does not usually perform poorly on the world stage. A combination of tough draws, bad luck, and low-scoring games has subverted its efforts. From 1974 to 1982, for example, Scotland put together a very respectable three-tournament record of three victories, two losses, and four ties. It scored sixteen goals and allowed fifteen. Yet it advanced in none of those tournaments, losing out on goal differential each time.

In 1986, Scotland was hurled, unmercifully, into "The Group of Death" with Uruguay, West Germany, and Denmark. Again, Scotland accounted itself well, and got absolutely nowhere. In 1990, just nine minutes from a scoreless tie with Brazil and a place in the second round, the Scots erred defensively and gave up the game-winning goal. Coach Andy Roxburgh was less than sportsmanlike in defeat, ripping fellow group member Costa Rica and complaining about scheduling problems. That night at the railway station in Turin, Italy, Scotland's kilt-clad fans behaved far more graciously, dancing into the early morning hours with the Brazilians, chanting in a conga line, "Come and join the polka."

Regardless of this international failure, Scotland's soccer is assured its place in history by the holy sporting wars between rival Glasgow club teams Celtic, with its Catholic supporters, and Rangers, with its Protestant backers. Graeme Souness, manager of the Rangers, became coach of the Scottish side in 1986, but like his predecessors—from Andrew Beatty to Ally MacLeod—was unable to unearth a striker who could turn opportunities into goals.

The Scottish style is, not unexpectedly, similar to its English cousins. With so many top Scots historically traveling south to play in England's first division, the evolution toward hard-tackle, long-pass soccer was inevitable. England has been more successful at its own invention only because it produced the more imaginative attackers. Defensively, Scotland has been England's equal.

SPAIN

THERE WAS PERHAPS NO GREATER HUMILIATION HEAPED UPON A soccer nation than what Spain's National Team dumped on its own doorstep in 1982. Host to the World Cup, seemingly well prepared by Uruguayan-born coach Jose Santamaria, Spain was fully expected to make a major impact on the tournament, if not win the whole affair. Instead, Spain did not survive to the quarterfinals. It scored a paltry four goals in five games, winning many unofficial awards from journalists for dull, uninspired play. The nation looked at its soccer self in the mirror, recoiled, and replaced the coach.

What followed was something of a modest success story, as new coach Miguel Muñoz built a strong foundation around his back line, and came within a shootout defeat by Belgium of reaching the semifinals in 1986 at Mexico. That team survived several hardships, including a virus that knocked out two stars, Gallego and Rafael Gordillo, from a first-round match against Brazil. A 5–1 victory over powerful, colorful Denmark in the quarterfinals was highlight enough to heal some old wounds back home, at least for another four years. Today, Spanish soccer appears relatively healthy again, and Luis Suarez' team won its tough group in the 1990 World Cup

TODAY, SPANISH SOCCER APPEARS RELATIVELY HEALTHY AGAIN, AND THE COUNTRY EASILY QUALIFIED FOR THE 1990 WORLD CUP WITH AN IMPRESSIVE WINNING STREAK.

before falling, 2–1, in the second round to Yugoslavia.

Spain's historic need for a consistent finisher has always been a bit puzzling, because the Spanish players are not without a certain flair and the swift Emilio Butragueno was capable, in that one 1986 match against Denmark, of scoring four goals. Consistent scoring, however, is another matter. Spain's soccer moguls—owners of world-class Real Madrid and Barcelona, for example—traditionally have poured their resources into importing offensive talent instead of developing their own. Too often in the past, Spain has been satisfied with producing top defenders like Victor Muñoz, and with tight, low-scoring matches that are too often 50–50 affairs.

SWEDEN

Although not often in the World Cup spotlight, Sweden scored its share of goals. Here, Swedish player Larssen celebrates a goal in a World Cup qualifying match.

IT WOULD BE COMFORTING TO SWEDISH SOCCER BUFFS IF ONLY A definitive historic moment could be found when things began to unravel; if there had been an aborted revolution, perhaps, as there was in Hungary.

Instead, the Swedes must look more to the Czech model of slow soccer disintegration. Like Czechoslovakia, Sweden is a high-latitude nation that gradually turned toward ice hockey and tennis, and away from soccer. It failed to qualify for the World Cups in 1982 and 1986, and hasn't really impacted on the tournament since it was the runner-up host in 1958. In 1990, after a nice qualifying run, the Swedes, under Olle Nordin, finished a humbling last in Group C, losing matches to Brazil, Scotland, and Costa Rica.

These days, Sweden's top professionals are bound to show up playing in Portugal, Italy, or anywhere else they can escape the high taxes at home. This creates the usual problems of gathering the stars together for qualifying matches, then expecting them to play in an organized fashion.

It wasn't always like this. Following a strong third-place showing in Brazil in 1950, Sweden was awarded the World Cup site in 1958 and promptly extended an amnesty of sorts to its pro players everywhere: Return home, and you can reap glory for the home side. Coach George Raynor returned from Italy for this great occasion, as did the brilliant, aging front line of Gunnar Gren, Gunnar Nordahl, and Niels Liedholm. Their skills were more delicate than those usually associated with European soccer, and it appeared they had placed a special stamp on the future of the game in Sweden by the time they finally yielded, 5–2, to Brazil in the 1958 final.

But the next generation of World Cuppers was more ordinary, its skills not as polished. Alas, the great Swedes of the fifties had been a bright, artistic flash in the pan.

UNITED STATES

IN AMERICA'S LONG, UNGLAMOROUS SOCCER HISTORY, THERE HAVE been two goals that stood above the rest: one by Joe Gaetjens that beat England 1–0 in 1950, and one thirty-nine years later by surprise starter Paul Caligiuri against Trinidad and Tobago that allowed the United States to qualify for the 1990 World Cup.

The United States was in the first World Cup in 1930 at Uruguay, but it was hardly an American team that made it to the semifinals that year. The starting eleven included five former Scottish pros and an Englishman, nicknamed "the shotputters" by some French journalists who were dismayed by their physical brand of football. From 1934 to 1947, the United States Soccer Federation decided to skip international competition, and paid a heavy price for it. Soccer stagnated as American football took charge of America's autumn sporting scene.

It was another Scotsman, Penn State coach Bill Jeffrey, who put together the 1950 World Cup team that upset England. This club included five players from St. Louis, Missouri, and only three foreign-born Americans (Gaetjens, a native Haitian, was one). While the victory over England was internationally dramatic and uplifting, the impact was virtually nonexistent back home. The United States national team struggled to a 2–11 record in full internationals during the fifties, then suffered some humiliating defeats to Norway (11–0), England (10–0), Italy (10–0), and Yugoslavia (9–1). Professional leagues, like the International Soccer League and the North American Soccer League, came and went in the States. They did nothing to promote the national team, and the advent of indoor soccer eroded the skills of top players like Ricky Davis. Worst, the Americans were grouped with Mexico in the CONCACAF World

Defender Steve Trittschuh of the United States (right) tackles Tomas Skuhravy during the 5–1 Czech victory. Skuhravy scored three goals, but Trittschuh was the big winner, signing a professional contract with Sparta of Prague.

Mike Windischmann (left) marks Giuseppe Giannini during the Americans' respectable 1-0 loss in Rome in World Cup '90.

With your feet, guys, not with your hands: United States coach Bob Gansler lectures his young players during an educational loss to Italy.

Cup qualifying region, and were unable to advance into the finals until Mexico's disqualification in 1989 and Caligiuri's shocking goal.

In that dramatic November 1989 match at Port-of-Spain, Trinidad, before 35,000 red-attired supporters of the T&T "Strike Squad," Caligiuri volleyed a twenty-five-yard (23-m) left-footer past keeper Michael Maurice in the thirty-first minute to quiet the calypso music in the stands. T&T had needed only a tie at home to go to Italy. Instead, it lost its dream, 1–0.

"This goal might be even bigger than ours was," said Walter Bahr, the halfback who assisted on Gaetjens' goal in 1950 and helped celebrate in 1989 amid the champagne and Budweiser in the winners' locker room. "We didn't realize how big ours was until about twenty years later."

At the World Cup in Italy, the Americans were overawed and overmatched against the Czechs in their opener at Florence, losing 5–1. They righted themselves somewhat, falling 1–0, respectably, to Italy, and 2–1 to Austria. In defeat, forward Caligiuri and midfielder Tab Ramos distinguished themselves.

The United States style of play under national coach Bob Gansler—not expected to last until 1994—has been a conservative mix of European styles, predominately English and German. The American brand of soccer is not quite up to those models, however. They lack ball control, flair, and a world-class striker. They went 238 minutes during World Cup qualifying matches without scoring a goal. Still, the United States is a fit squad, with strong tacklers and excellent goaltending depth in Tony Meola and David Vanole. They are young, and have had great success recently in under-twenty and under-sixteen internationals. Under Gansler in 1988, the under-twenties finished fourth in the world in a tournament at Saudi Arabia.

So there is hope, albeit for the distant future, well beyond the United States World Cup in 1994.

URUGUAY

FOR A TINY NATION WITH A TOTAL POPULATION LESS THAN THE CITY of Boston, Massachusetts, Uruguay has a glorious soccer history that extends to the very beginnings of the sport. The country's grassroots support landed them the first World Cup in 1930, which they went on to win at Montevideo. Uruguay won again in 1950, in a huge upset on Brazilian turf.

"Other countries have their history," said Ondino Viera, Uruguay's coach in 1966. "Uruguay has its football."

Uruguay's soccer has had its ups and downs, following in part the country's own economic ebbs and flows. Declines in the 1950s and 1960s encouraged its stars to look elsewhere—many toward Europe—to enhance their careers. Even before then, there had been extended player strikes and defections. When those players finally returned to the national team, it was often on a short-term basis that did not allow for unifying practices.

The playing style of Los Celestes (The Sky Blues, the color of the Uruguayan team shirts and the stripes on the country's flag) is unique in South America. Particularly over the last two decades, Uruguay has gone to more physical European tactics, depending less on the flair of one or two stars and more on the mechanizations of the whole. A talented but flawed Uruguay reached the second round at Italia '90 on a dramatic, last-minute goal against South Korea, then lost a tough 1–0 match to host Italy.

"We cannot play like Brazilians," said coach Omar Borras during the 1986 World Cup in Mexico. "We have a South American style with more strength to it, a more practical game."

That "strength" has sometimes overstepped accepted boundaries, as it did at the 1986 World Cup. Then, Uruguayan players were red-carded in matches against Denmark and Scotland, and were whistled for thirty-three fouls during a game against Argentina. At least nobody has ever accused Uruguay of indifference.

Enzo Francescoli heads downfield in this 1990 World Cup qualifying match.

Uruguay, the first World Cup champs, in 1930: Alvaro Gestido, Jose Mazassi, Enrique Ballestrero, Ernesto Masqueroni, Jose Leandre Andrade, Lorenzo Fernandez, Pablo Dorado, Hector Scarone, Hector Casstro, Pedro Cea, and Santos Iriarte.

WEST GERMANY

Lothar Matthaeus couldn't break down the British defense in this 1990 semifinal match, but no matter. The West Germans went on to win in a shootout.

IT IS NO ACCIDENT THAT THE WEST GERMANS HAVE AMASSED THE most successful World Cup record of any nation over the past thirty-six years: five finals and three championships, including the 1990 World Cup title in Italy. The Germans are talented, but their consistency (a fifty-two-year-old unbeaten streak in World Cup qualifiers from 1933 to 1985 remains one of soccer's more amazing feats) derives from a combination of factors, including style, organization, and economics.

The Germans have known only a few national coaches. There have been no managerial juggling acts, which seem to haunt the South American soccer federations. Sepp Herberger, a sharp tactician and inspirational motivator, was manager-selector from 1938 to 1962. He eventually gave way to Helmut Schoen, who won the 1974 World Cup in Munich, using many of Herberger's methods. After Jupp Derwall, Franz Beckenbauer moved from midfield to the sideline. Again, the style of play was not overtly affected. *"Wir mussen Deutschspielen"* (We must be German), Beckenbauer said.

Being German in soccer means playing one of the best-rounded games in the world. Quickness is critical, because the attack is mounted from midfield, with players bunching on the ball and isolating off the ball to create gaps and passing chances. Defense is man-to-man, so individual speed is a requisite.

Because the German professional league (the Bundesliga) is successful and financially top-rung, the country's best players usually remain at or near home (certainly, no farther away than Italy) during the soccer season. This makes selection for the national team relatively convenient, and greatly advantageous. The players know each other, and often have been teammates on clubs like Bayern Munich. German World Cup teams, as a whole, have been better than their parts—and as the Germans showed in 1990, parts like Rudi Voeller, Lothar Matthaeus, and Juergen Klinsmann are golden in their own way.

Although the retirement of Beckenbauer will slow things down a bit, the Germans appear set for years to come. The reunification of the country figures to make the team even stronger, with the expected addition of three or four top-notch East Germans.

"The Germans will not be beatable," predicted Beckenbauer. "That is bad news for the rest of the world."

© David Cannon/Allsport

YUGOSLAVIA

PERHAPS REFLECTING THIS COUNTRY'S ICONOCLASTIC POLITICS, THE Yugoslav soccer team historically has presented an individualistic mixture of styles and creative play not usually demonstrated by the Eastern bloc. Young midfielder Dragan Stojkovic, his sunglasses and detached bemusement a World Cup fixture in Italy, embodied this rebellious success at the 1990 World Cup, where Yugoslavia defeated Spain and advanced to the quarterfinals.

Yugoslavia began making big noises during the Olympics of 1952 in Helsinki, where it knocked out Russia 3–1. It reached the quarterfinals of the 1954 World Cup in Switzerland, the quarterfinals of the 1958 World Cup in Sweden, and the semifinals of the 1962 World Cup in Chile, where Jerkovic led all scorers with five goals.

This decade of excellence began with a special crop of elegant attackers in the middle of the field: Milos Milutinovic, Dragolsav Sekularac, and Branko Zebec. In goal was the wonderfully graceful Vladimir Beara, a formal disciple of ballet.

By 1962, this core group, plus or minus a few players, was one of the favorites to win the World Cup in Chile. Team manager Milovan Ciric, no tyrant, used a modified 4–2–4 structure, giving his players more positional freedom than usual. "English methods are always so rigid," he reportedly complained. "They must improvise more. Why must it always be wing-half to inside-left, inside-left to outside-right, then a cross?"

The Yugoslavs improvised their way to the semifinals, where they met their match in Czechoslovakia, something of a mirror image of the Yugoslavs, with a hotter goaltender. Yugoslavia lost 3–1 and went until 1990 before coach Ivan Osim and players like Stojkovic recovered some of that lost glory.

Dragan Stojkovic, Yugoslavia's showstopper, dissects Colombia during a 1–0 win in the 1990 World Cup. Stojkovic was rewarded with a multi-million dollar contract by Olympique Marseille.

Soccer's Future in the U.S.

A few American fans traveled 7,000 miles to Italy to watch their nation compete in its first World Cup in many years. Will more be interested in 1994, when the sacred tournament arrives at their shores?

WHEN THE EXECUTIVE COMMITTEE OF FIFA VOTED IN 1988 to award the 1994 World Cup to the eternal soccer ingrates in the United States, there was considerable protest from aficionados abroad.

"What justification is there for awarding the 1994 World Cup to a country with no conceivable chance of winning it?" wrote columnist Ken Jones of the *Independent* in London. "One in which the most international game is still regarded as a curiosity."

Jones was right, to a degree. The United States certainly has no chance whatsoever of winning the 1994 World Cup, and the majority of middle-aged residents from the redwood forests to the New York harbor wouldn't know a soccer ball from a beach ball. And yet the decision was a logical one for FIFA, which is trying to tap a potentially grand, lucrative market that produced a $225 million profit for the Los Angeles Olympics.

Consider that by last year, there were more than ten million soccer players in America. Youth teams abound, and the under-sixteen national club has been tremendously successful, even world class, in top international competitions.

"The game is now embedded in the culture, played by so many kids, encouraged by so many parents who do not know that soccer used to be a funny foreign game," said Clive Toye, the soccer promoter who once helped bring Pelé to the New York Cosmos.

This does not mean that the future of soccer is assured in the United States, or even that the World Cup itself will be an automatic success. While Americans now enjoy watching their children play this vigorous, healthy sport, they have yet to show much enthusiasm for attending top-flight matches, or watching them on television. They seem to lack the concentration span for it, requiring sports like baseball and football that cue them into the action with structured mini-dramas like innings (baseball) and downs (American football). With soccer, they don't know when to get their beer from the fridge and networks don't know when to put on commercials. All this makes everyone uncomfortable.

Still, America is diverse, and it is wealthy. There is a base of ethnic support guaranteed for many teams—the South American nations, Mexico, and Italy, to name a few. In addition, the two countries bidding against the United States to host the 1994 World Cup had substantial problems. Morocco would have had to build nine new stadiums to fulfill FIFA's minimum requirements, and Brazilian stadiums need major overhauls.

So 1994 will bring the first World Cup in which the host team—the United States qualifies automatically—would create a major stir simply by surviving the first round and enduring to the "Sweet Sixteen." It is a strange scenario, but perhaps the fairest one yet. Super clubs of the past, teams like Hungary in 1954 and Holland in 1974, were victimized by the home field disadvantage. In a more equitable setting, it could be argued the best team has a better shot at winning.

PLANNING FOR 1994

THE NUTS-AND-BOLTS PLANNING FOR THE 1994 WORLD CUP IS BEING handled by the Organizing Committee, tentatively under the direction of President Scott LeTellier, in accordance with FIFA. LeTellier is very corporate, unable to relate well with the international community. For this reason alone, FIFA pressured the Organizing Committee and the U.S. Soccer Federation to accept some outside help or make overtures to the popular, respected Franz Beckenbauer. After some initial resistance·–"Ultimately, this is our show," former USSF President Werner Fricker said—the Organizing Committee recruited Beckenbauer and others.

In August 1990, FIFA-backed candidate Alan Rothenberg unseated Fricker as president of the USSF. Rothenberg, former owner of the chaotic Los Angeles Clippers of the National Basketball Association, had organized soccer events at the 1984 Olympics.

The dates and sites of the tournament had not yet been determined at press time, but the Organizing Committee was able to give a general overview of the tournament.

The opening ceremonies will take place in June, probably on a Friday, and the final will be played on a Sunday in July. As many as twelve stadiums throughout the country will serve as venues for the twenty-four teams. Most of those sites will come from the list of seventeen potential hosts that supported the Soccer Federation's application for the World Cup. Here is that list, with stadium capacity:

· Arrowhead Stadium, Kansas City, Missouri 78,067 · Citrus Bowl, Orlando, Florida, 50,000 · Cotton Bowl, Dallas, Texas, 72,000 · Franklin Field, Philadelphia, Pennsylvania, 60,546 · Husky Stadium, Seattle, Washington, 72,000 · Joe Robbie Stadium, Fort Lauderdale, Florida, 75,500 · Memorial Coliseum, Los Angeles, California, 92,000 · Minnesota Sports Complex, Blaine, Minnesota, 45,000 · Navy-Marine Corps Stadium, Annapolis, Maryland, 30,000 · Orange Bowl, Miami, Florida, 75,500 · Palmer Stadium, Princeton, New Jersey, 45,000 · Parker, Corvallis, Oregon, 40,593 · Robert F. Kennedy, Washington, D.C., 57,000 · Rose Bowl, Pasadena, California, 104,091 · Silver Bowl, Las Vegas, Nevada, 32,000 · Soldier Field, Chicago, Illinois, 66,814 · Tampa, Tampa, Florida, 74,317.

Soldier Field, in Chicago, is one of the prospective host sites for the 1994 World Cup.

A few of these stadiums have artificial surfaces, and will have to be converted to grass by tournament time. In addition, the Yale Bowl in New Haven, Connecticut; Stanford Stadium in Palo Alto, California; and Michigan Stadium in Ann Arbor, among others, have expressed interest in playing host. Also, FIFA, to the dismay of many soccer purists, gave its tentative approval in 1990 to the idea of playing matches in indoor stadiums. This opened the door to new applicants, with potential sites such as the Hoosier Dome in Indianapolis; the Silverdome in Pontiac, Michigan; the Carrier Dome, in Syracuse, New York; the Superdome in New Orleans, Louisiana; the Astrodome in Houston, Texas; the TacomaDome, in Washington; and the MetroDome in Minneapolis, Minnesota.

Other potential changes that FIFA has hinted at have also scared the purists. João Havelange has mentioned the possibility of breaking the matches into four, twenty-five-minute quarters, for the benefit of television broadcasts. The 1990 World Cup was such a failure on American television—watched by a paltry 2 percent share on TNT cable network—that FIFA is figuring out a way to get some United States commercial network interested in the 1994 broadcast rights. Of the three networks, only CBS appeared even remotely intrigued by such possibilities.

Rumors that the United States would pull out of the 1994 bid because of problems with corporate sponsors appear to be spurious. In late 1992 or early 1993, ticket orders will be made available throughout the United States at outlets such as retail stores or banks. The identities of the twenty-four participating teams will be known after qualifying matches are completed in November 1993, and a draw that December will decide which nations play in which venues.

While the United States Soccer Federation fell on hard financial times during its expensive qualifying run for the 1990 World Cup in Italy, the Organizing Committee remained on solid fiscal ground due to large donations from the World Cup USA Founders Club and several corporate bid supporters. Since FIFA controls the sale of all international sponsorships and television rights in 1994, the Organizing Committee's chief source of revenue will be ticket sales. It is unlikely there will be much money to divvy up afterwards with the United States Soccer Federation.

At least forty of the games will be televised live in the United States. But there will be no avoiding those insipid commercials—and those missed goals these intrusive ads inevitably block. Overseas, of course, things will be far more civilized and telegenic. As far as security goes, the Organizing Committee is hopeful that the lack of standing room in host stadiums around the United States will avoid many of the problems that have plagued European and South American matches. A seated hooligan doesn't pack quite the wallop of a standing hoodlum. If visiting fans want to make a scene at an American train station, they will discover that there are few witnesses to impress with their outlandish behavior; except in major East Coast cities, Americans do not take the train. They drive cars. Freeways make for lousy riot sites.

WHY THE UNITED STATES?

THE REASON THE UNITED STATES SOCCER FEDERATION BID SO HARD for the World Cup was not because it believed the American team had much of a chance of emerging as champions. "It must be clear that while winning the World Cup is the ultimate goal of any Federation development program, other goals and targets must also be set and realized," said Werner Fricker, former president of the Federation.

Fricker is a Hungarian expatriate whose anti-communist zeal borders on the fanatic (it is still rumored that he took all the red out of the Americans' red, white, and blue uniforms for political reasons, though Fricker denies this) and whose pro-Americanism is just as emphatic. He was hopeful that the Cup would inject some real interest—and money—into the sport on a national basis. Most important, he wanted a thoroughly established professional league and guaranteed employment for top American players by the completion of the tournament. The USSF's failure to establish such a league probably cost Fricker his job.

For a while in 1989, it appeared that all of the dreams would die a slow fiscal death. The Federation fell into debt during the qualification run for Italy, overspending by nearly $1 million in salaries and travel expenses. Fortunately, Paul Caligiuri scored a goal in Port-of-Spain, Trinidad, on November 19, 1989, and the United States qualified for the World Cup. Beyond $1.4 million in direct revenues from Italy, this meant an outpouring of commercial sponsorship that some officials estimated could reach $10 million. Suddenly, there was momentum—and financing—for Rothenberg and 1994.

All-Time World Cup Standings · 1930–1990

NATION	G	W	L	T	PT.	GF	GA	TITLES
1. Brazil	66	44	11	11	99	148	65	3
2. West Germany	68	40	14	14	94	145	90	3
3. Italy	54	31	12	11	73	89	54	3
4. Argentina	48	26	15	7	59	82	59	2
5. England	41	18	12	11	47	55	38	1
6. Uruguay	37	15	14	8	38	61	52	2
7. USSR	31	15	10	6	36	53	34	0
8. France	34	15	14	5	35	71	56	0
9. Yugoslavia	33	14	13	6	34	55	42	0
10. Hungary	32	15	14	3	33	87	57	0
11. Spain	32	13	12	7	33	43	38	0
12. Poland	25	13	7	5	31	39	29	0
13. Sweden	31	11	14	6	28	51	52	0
14. Czechoslovakia	30	11	14	5	27	44	45	0
15. Austria	26	12	12	2	26	40	43	0
16. Netherlands	20	8	6	6	22	35	23	0
17. Belgium	25	7	14	4	18	33	49	0
18. Mexico	29	6	17	6	18	27	64	0
19. Chile	21	7	11	3	17	26	32	0
20. Scotland	20	4	10	6	14	23	35	0
21. Portugal	9	6	3	0	12	19	12	0
22. Switzerland	18	5	11	2	12	28	44	0
23. Northern Ireland	13	3	5	5	11	13	23	0
24. Peru	15	4	8	3	11	19	31	0
25. Paraguay	11	3	4	4	10	16	25	0
26. Cameroon	8	3	2	3	9	8	9	0
27. Romania	12	3	7	2	8	16	20	0
28. Denmark	4	3	1	0	6	10	6	0
29. East Germany	6	2	2	2	6	5	5	0
30. United States	10	3	7	0	6	14	29	0
31. Bulgaria	16	0	10	6	6	11	35	0
32. Wales	5	1	1	3	5	4	4	0
33. Ireland	5	1	1	3	5	2	3	0
34. Morocco	7	1	3	3	5	5	8	0
35. Algeria	6	2	3	1	5	6	10	0
36. Costa Rica	4	2	2	0	4	4	6	0
37. Colombia	7	1	4	2	4	9	15	0
38. Tunisia	3	1	1	1	3	3	2	0
39. North Korea	4	1	2	1	3	5	9	0
40. Cuba	3	1	1	1	3	5	12	0
41. Turkey	3	1	2	0	2	10	11	0
42. Honduras	3	0	1	2	2	2	3	0
43. Israel	3	0	1	2	2	1	3	0
44. Egypt	4	0	2	2	2	3	6	0
45. Kuwait	3	0	2	1	1	2	6	0
46. Australia	3	0	2	1	1	0	5	0
47. Iran	3	0	2	1	1	2	8	0
48. South Korea	8	0	7	1	1	5	29	0
49. Norway	1	0	1	0	0	1	2	0
50. Iraq	3	0	3	0	0	1	4	0
51. Canada	3	0	3	0	0	0	5	0
52. Netherlands East Indies	1	0	1	0	0	0	6	0
53. United Arab Emirates	3	0	3	0	0	2	11	0
54. New Zealand	3	0	3	0	0	2	12	0
55. Haiti	3	0	3	0	0	2	14	0
56. Zaire	3	0	3	0	0	0	14	0
57. Bolivia	3	0	3	0	0	0	16	0
58. El Salvador	6	0	6	0	0	1	22	0

Leading Scorers · 1930–1990

YEAR	PLAYER	GAMES	GOALS
1930	Guillermo Stabile, *Argentina*	4	8
1934	Angelo Schiavio, *Italy*	3	4
	Oldrich Nejedly, *Czechoslovakia*	4	4
	Edmund Conen, *Germany*	4	4
1938	Leonidas, *Brazil*	3	8
1950	Ademir, *Brazil*	6	7
1954	Sandor Kocsis, *Hungary*	5	11
1958	Just Fontaine, *France*	6	13
1962	Drazen Jerkovic, *Yugoslavia*	6	5
1966	Eusebio, *Portugal*	6	9
1970	Gerd Muller, *West Germany*	6	10
1974	Grzegorz Lato, *Poland*	7	7
1978	Mario Kempes, *Argentina*	7	6
1982	Paolo Rossi, *Italy*	7	6
1986	Gary Lineker, *England*	5	6
1990	Salvatore Schillaci, *Italy*	7	6

Further Reading

Batty, Eric G. *Soccer Coaching, the European Way.* New York: Dial Press, 1980.

Chyzowych, Walter, *The World Cup.* South Bend, Indiana: Icarus Press, 1982.

Glanville, Brian. *The History of the World Cup.* London: Faber and Faber, 1984.

Glanville, Brian. *Soccer; History of the Game, Its Players and Its Strategy.* New York: Crown, 1968.

Henshaw, Richard. *Encyclopedia of World Soccer.* Washington, D.C.: New Republic Books, 1979.

Hill, Jimmy. *Great Soccer Stars.* London: Hamlyn, 1978.

Kowet, Don. *Pelé (Edson Arantes do Nascimento).* New York: Atheneum/SMI, 1976.

Rollin, Jack. *Guinness Book of Soccer Facts and Feats.* Middlesex, England: Guinness Superlatives, Ltd., 1978.

Rollin, Jack. *Soccer; Records, Facts, and Champions.* Enfield, England: Guinness, 1988.

INDEX

Page numbers in italics refer to captions and illustrations. Page numbers in boldface refer to biographies of specific players.

Amarildo, 21, *21*
Anbari, Abdul al-, *34*
Andrade, Jose, 9, *119*
Anni, Robert, *14*
Arantes do Nascimento, Edson. See Pelé
Argentina (1978), 31–33
Argentina (team), 100
Aston, Ken, 21

Bahr, Walter, 14, *14*, 118
Ballestrero, Enrique, *119*
Banks, Gordon, 22, *24*, **50–51**
Barlson, *22*
Battiston, Patrick, *34*, *35*, 36, *93*, **94**
Bearzot, Enzo, 92, 110
Beckenbauer, Franz, 23, 44, 46, 49, **51–52**, 74, 75, *78*, 80, 94, *112*, 120, 123
Belgium (team), 101
Bergoni, Giuseppe, *37*
Bertoni, Daniel, 33, 65
Bilardo, Carlos, 44–45, 65, 100
Biyik, Omam, 42, *43*
Bliard, Rene, 18, 60
Boniek, Zbigniew, 69, 114
Borghi, Frank, *14*
Borja, Enrique, *111–12*
Bozsik, Josef, 15, 67, 109
Brazil (1950), 13–15
Brazil (team), 102–3
Brehme, Andreas, 44–45
Buckley, Frank, 84

Caligiuri, Paul, 117–18, 126
Canada (team), 103
Caniggia, Claudio, 43–44, *73*
Carnovali, *28*
Castro, Hector, 10, *119*
Cea, Pedro, 9, *9*, 10, *119*
Charlton, Bobby, 22, 23, 52, *54*, **54–55**, 107
Chile (1962), 20–21
Codesal, Edgardo, 45
Cohen, George, 22
Colombo, Charles, *14*
Combs, Jeff, *14*
Continho, 31, 102
Cruyff, Johann, 28, *28*, 29, 32, **55–56**, *56*, 81, 89, 112, *112*

Czechoslovakia (team), 104–5
Czeizler, Lajor, 84

Da Silva, Leonidas.
    See Leonidas
Denmark (team), 105–6
Didi, *102*, 84
Didi, 18, *57*, **57–58**, 61
Di Stefano, Alfredo, 49, 58, 88
Dorado, Pablo, *119*

Edinho, 102
Elkjaer-Larsen, Preben, 105–6
England (1966), 22–24
England (team), 106–7
Eusebio, **58–60**, *59*, 80, 88

Falcao, Paulo, *90*, *91*
Federation Internationale des Football Associations (FIFA), 7–8
Felix, 25, 65
Feola, Vincente, 18, 58, 102
Fernandez, Lorenzo, 9, *9*, *119*
Fontaine, Just, 18, 49, *60*, **60–61**
France (1938), 12–13
France (team), 108
Francescoli, Enzo, *119*
Francisco dos Santos, Manuel.
    See Garrincha

Gadocha, Robert, *68*
Gaetjens, Joe, 14, *14*, 117–18
Gansler, Bob, 118, *118*
Gardassanish, Gino, *14*
Garrincha, 21, *21*, 22, 49, 58, *61*, **61–62**, *102*
Gascoigne, Paul, *62*, **62–63**, 106
Germany, West (1974), 28–30
Germany, West (team), 120
Gestido, Alvaro, 9, *119*
Giannini, Giuseppe, *118*
Glockner, Rudi, 56
Goycoechea, Sergio, *44*, 44–45, *64*, **64–65**
Graddock, Robert, *14*
Greenwood, Ron, 79
Gren, Gunnar, 18, 116–17
Grosics, Gyula, 16, *17*
Gullit, Ruud, 112–13

Hidalgo, Michel, 86, 108
Hidegkuti, Nandor, 109
Higuita, Rene, 77
Hungary (team), 109
Hurst, Geoff, 23, *23*, 79

Iriarte, Santos, 10, *119*
Italy (1934), 10–11
Italy (1990), 42–46
Italy (team), 110–11

Jaairzinho, 25, 51
Jacobs, Ditmar, 41
Jeffy, Bill, *14*
Jezek, Vaclav, 105
Jongbloed, Jan, *32*, 66

Kempes, Mario, 33, *33*, *65*, **65–66**, *66*, 97
Keough, Harry, 14, *14*
Klinsmann, Juergen, 45–46, 74–75, 120
Kocsis, Sandor, 15, *67*, **67–68**, 87, 109
Kopa, Raymond, 18, 60

Larssen, 116
Lato, Grzegorz, *68*, **68–69**
Laudrup, Michael, 105–6
Leonidas, **69–70**, 87, 102
Liebrich, Werner, 16, 87
Liedholm, Niels, 116–17
Lineker, Gary, 41, 44, 49, *70*, **70–72**, *71*, *72*
Lyon, Chubby, *14*

Maca, Joe, *14*
McKinnon, 22
MacLeod, Ally, 31–32, 115
Maier, Sepp, 29, *29*, 69
Male, George, 84, *84*
Mandi, Gyula, 109
Maradona, Diego, 31, **38–41**, *39*, 42, 44–45, *45*, 65–66, **72–74**, *73*, 75, 84, 93, 100, *100*
Masopust, Josef, 21, 105
Masqueroni, Ernesto, *119*
Matthaeus, Lothar, 39, 46, 74, **74–75**, 120, *120*
Matthews, Stanley, *75*, **75–76**, *76*
Mazassi, Jose, *119*
Mexico (1970), 25–27
Mexico (1986), 38–41
Mexico (team), 111–12
Michel, Henri, 108
Michels, Rinus, 56, 112
Milla, Roger, 43, 77, *77*
Milutinovic, Milos, 112, 121
Molanin, Adal, *14*
Moore, Bobby, 22, 25, 50, 61, *78*, **78–79**, *79*, 82, 107
Muller, Gerd, *25*, 29, *80*, **80–81**
Munoz, Victor, 116

Neeskens, Johan, 29, *30*, 66, 81, *81*, 112
Netherlands (team), 112–13

Nilto, 61
Nordahl, Gunnar, 116–17
Nordin, Ollie, 116

Orio, Nick D., *14*
Orsi, Raimondo, 11, 87

Pak Doo Ik, 22
Pariani, Gino, *14*
Pelé, 18, *18*, 21, 22, *22*, 25, 27, *27*, 28, 49, 50, *50*, 51, 57, 58–60, 61, *61*, 65, 67, 70, 72, 74, 79, 80, *82*, **82–83**, *83*, 84, 86, 102–3, 122
Pereira, Valdir. See Didi
Perez, Luis Alonso, 82–83
Pfaff, Jean-Marie, 101
Piola, Silvio, 12–13, *84*, **84**
Planicka, Franticek, 11, 12, **86–87**, *88*, 105
Platini, Michel, *34*, 49, 72, 84, *85*, **85–86**, 108, *108*
Platt, 44
Poland (team), 113–14
Polleunis, Odilon, 101
Pozzo, Vittorio, 11, 12, *12*, 13, 84, 110
Pumpido, Nery, 42, 64, 65
Puskas, Ferenc, 15–16, 49, 67, **87–88**

Quinn, Niall, *42*

Rahn, Helmut, 16, *17*
Raiman, *104*
Ramsey, Alf, 22, 50, 79, *106*, **106–7**
Resenbrink, Rob, 29, 33, 112
Rijkaard, Fank, 112–13
Rimet, Jules, 8, 27, 87
Riva, Luigi, 27, *88*, **88–89**, *89*, 90
Rivelino, Roberto, 25, 102
Rivera, Gianni, 27, 88, **89–90**
Robson, Bobby, 44, 62, 106
Robson, Bryan, 62, 106
Roja, 21
Rossi, Paolo, 36, *90*, **90–92**, *91*, *92*, 110, *110*
Rummenigge, Karl-Heinz, 36, *37*, 39–41, **93–94**

Sagrini, Antonio, *36*
Sanchez, Hugo, 49, 112
Sanchez, Leonel, 20
Scarone, Hector, 9, *42*, *119*
Schaefer, Hans, 16, *17*
Schillaci, Salvatore, 43–44, 45, 75, 92, **92–93**, *110*
Schoen, Helmut, 23, 31, 120

Schumacher, Harald "Toni", *34*, **34–36**, 39–41, 92, *93*, **93–94**, *94*
Scifo, Vincenzo, 101, *101*
Scotland (team), 114–15
Serrizuela, Jose, 45
Skuhravy, Tomas, **94–95**, *95*
Souza, Ed, *14*
Souza, John, *14*
Spain (1982), 34–37
Spain (team), 115–16
Stabile, Guillermo, 9, **96**, *96*
Stojkovic, Dragan, 121
Sweden (1958), 18–19
Sweden (team), 116–17
Switzerland (1954), 15–17

Thys, Guy, 38, 101

United States, soccer's future in, 122–26
United States (team), 117–18
Uruguay (1930), 9–10
Uruguay (team), 119

Valcareggi, Feruccio, 28, 90
Valecenti, Frank, *14*
Van Basten, Marco, 112–13
Vava, 18, 21, *21*, 58, *102*
Vicini, Azeglio, 93, 111
Voeller, Rudi, 39–41, 45–46, 74, 75, 120
Vytlacil, Rudolf, 104–5

Weber, 23, *24*
Williams, Stuart, 18
Windischmann, Mike, 118
Winterbottom, Walter, 75–76
World Cup
    all-time standings, 127
    history and creation of, 8
    leading scorers, 127
    planning for 1994, 123–26
    See also specific World Cups indexed by country and date

Yugoslavia (team), 121

Zagalo, Mario Lobo, *102*
Zamora, Ricardo, 11, 86
Zenga, Walter, 43–44, 111
Zeze, 12, 102
Zoff, Dino, *96*, **96–97**